Teaching with Google Classroom

Put Google Classroom to work while teaching your students and make your life easier

Michael Zhang

BIRMINGHAM - MUMBAI

Teaching with Google Classroom

First published: September 2016

Production reference: 1270916

Published by Packt Publishing Ltd.
Livery Place
35 Livery Street
Birmingham
B3 2PB, UK.
ISBN 978-1-78646-628-0

www.packtpub.com

Credits

Author

Michael Zhang

Reviewer

Dr. Karen L. Sipe

Commissioning Editor

David Barnes

Acquisition Editors

Usha Iyer

Reshma Raman

Content Development Editor

Mehvash Fatima

Technical Editors

Bhagyashree Rai

Pratik Tated

Copy Editor

Tom Jacob

Project Coordinator

Kinjal Bari

Proofreader

Safis Editing

Indexer

Pratik Shirodkar

Graphics

Kirk D'Penha

Production Coordinator

Deepika Naik

About the Author

Michael Zhang is a certified trainer for Google Apps for Education. He has an Education and Science degree from the University of Alberta and works within the public school system in Canada. He is in contact with a large population of teachers and often questions them regarding modern technologies within the classroom. Given the opportunity, he teaches classes as well and has opportunities to use Google Apps for Education for a consistent set of students. Michael has spoken at several teaching conventions and facilitates technology training in Google Apps, Microsoft Office, Adobe Creative Cloud and other software. His experiences help him to communicate technology in a comprehensible manner to his audience. He believes that technology should save time and improve productivity and hopes this book does just that for its readers.

About the Reviewer

Dr. Karen L Sipe has a bachelor's degree from the York College of Pennsylvania in secondary education, a master's degree in school administration from McDaniel College, a doctoral degree from Immaculata University in school leadership and a post-master's degree from Philadelphia University as a technology specialist. She is a member of PAECT and ASCD.

Dr. Sipe has completed online course development training through Wilkes University in collaboration with the Pennsylvania Department of Education (PDE). She has developed online courses for PDE and facilitated online courses for Wilkes University.

In addition to her many responsibilities, Dr. Sipe maintains the CVSD Tech Tips blog in the district. Through the blog, she presents information about various technology tools and resources (`http://www.conewago.k12.pa.us/tech-tips-blog`).

Dr. Sipe has been with the Conewago Valley School District for 22 years. She was initially a teacher of business education, then a high school assistant principal, and for the last 12 years, she has held the position of Director of Educational Programs. Part of her responsibilities include the planning and implementation of technology-related professional development and coaching the K-12 staff.

Dr. Sipe is also an adjunct instructor for Wilson College in Chambersburg, Pennsylvania. She instructs graduate students on how to integrate technology into their classrooms.

As Director of Educational Services, she has led, for her employer, technology boot camps in collaboration with Neumann College in Aston, Pennsylvania.

Dr. Sipe is continually exploring new resources and tools that make the classroom more engaging and interactive for students and teachers. Her latest personal study is in the area of hybrid learning models and the incorporation and development of digital classrooms within these models.

> *I want to thank Packt for allowing me to be part of this editing process. This book is very well written and I believe will be very beneficial to those with an interest in becoming proficient in the use of Google Classroom.*

www.PacktPub.com

eBooks, discount offers, and more

Did you know that Packt offers eBook versions of every book published, with PDF and ePub files available? You can upgrade to the eBook version at www.PacktPub.com and as a print book customer, you are entitled to a discount on the eBook copy. Get in touch with us at customercare@packtpub.com for more details.

At www.PacktPub.com, you can also read a collection of free technical articles, sign up for a range of free newsletters and receive exclusive discounts and offers on Packt books and eBooks.

https://www.packtpub.com/mapt

Get the most in-demand software skills with Mapt. Mapt gives you full access to all Packt books and video courses, as well as industry-leading tools to help you plan your personal development and advance your career

Why subscribe?

- Fully searchable across every book published by Packt
- Copy and paste, print, and bookmark content
- On demand and accessible via a web browser

To my loving wife, who supported me in every step of the way. To my amazing sister and parents, who encouraged me to pursue this endeavor. To my editors and Packt Publishing, who believed I could write this book. To all my teaching colleagues who shared their ideas. Thank you all.

Table of Contents

Preface

Google Classroom is part of the Google Apps for Education (GAFE) suite of online productivity apps packaged for teachers and students for online learning and collaboration. It is free, but must be deployed at the educational institution level. While GAFE contains many popular Google Apps such as Gmail, Google Calendar, and Google Drive, that are accessible to anyone, Google Classroom is found only in GAFE. It provides a central site to communicate with students, assign homework, and send feedback. Some key strengths of Google Classroom are its time-saving features and easy-to-use and simple organization. Google Classroom is like a virtual extension of a brick-and-mortar classroom.

The book provides a comprehensive overview of how to set up Google Classroom and what features are available. It begins with creating classes and adding students. Then it explores the features found within Google Classroom such as sending announcements, starting discussions and distributing and collecting assignments. Later, the book explores how additional GAFE integrate with Google Classroom to grade assignments faster and connect with parents. Each chapter contains examples, screenshots with step-by-step instructions, and anecdotal experience gained during my time teaching with Google Classroom.

What this book covers

This book is about using Google Classroom effectively so that it helps organize your classes and saves you time. It first covers all the features within Google Classroom, and then includes third-party extensions and other Google Apps to enhance Google Classroom's features. Each chapter provides in-depth instructions to set up Google Classroom and these third-party extensions in a step-by-step fashion.

Chapter 1, *Getting to Know Google Classroom,* is an introduction to the layout and features within Google Classroom. It prepares classes for the subsequent chapters. By the end of this chapter, the reader will be able create a class in Google Classroom, change its theme, and add files.

Chapter 2, *Inviting Students to Their Virtual Classroom,* introduces students to Google Classroom. It covers adding students to their class and connecting their devices to Google Classroom. By the end of this chapter, the reader will be able to instruct students in joining a class, add students directly to a class, and access Google Classroom on desktop and mobile devices.

Chapter 3, *Sending Your First Announcement,* provides the first foray into interacting with students within Google Classroom. It explores the class Stream and the features of the Announcement post. By the end of this chapter, the reader will be able to send announcements to students within Google Classroom.

Chapter 4, *Starting an Online Discussion with Questions,* explores the second post type within the class Stream—Questions. It covers asking discussion questions and providing peer and teacher feedback to student answers. By the end of this chapter, the reader will be able to assign a question, provide feedback, and assign a grade to the students' answers.

Chapter 5, *Handing out and Taking in Assignments,* will focus on attaching files to assignment posts and best practices in file types and distributing assignments within Google Classroom. It includes instructions for guiding students to submit completed assignments and setting a due date. By the end of this chapter, the reader will be able to add a file to an assignment, distribute it to students, and teach students to submit finished work.

Chapter 6, *Grading Written Assignments in a Flash,* is the first chapter to explore third-party apps and extensions that enhance the features of Google Classroom. This chapter covers the built-in grading features, then uses Doctopus and Goobric to grade written assignments. By the end of this chapter, the reader will be able to set up Doctopus and Goobric and grade written assignments with a rubric.

Chapter 7, *Google Forms for Multiple Choice and Fill-in-the-Blank Assignments,* continues from the previous chapter. It focuses on creating multiple choice and fill-in-the-blanks questions using Google Forms and automatically grading the assignments with Flubaroo. By the end of this chapter, the reader will be able to create an assignment in Google Forms, assign it in Google Classroom, install, and set up Flubaroo to autograde the assignment.

Chapter 8, *Keeping Parents in the Loop,* addresses Google Classroom's inability to grant access to parents and others who do not have a Google Apps for Education account. It explains how Google Classroom's assignments are connected to Google Calendar. It provides strategies in sharing the Google Calendar so that parents can view assignment deadlines and other important information. By the end of this chapter, the reader will be able to share a Google Calendar using a URL or in a Google Site.

Chapter 9, *Customizing to Your Subject,* provides subject-specific examples of third-party apps, add-ons, and extensions that diversifies the types of online assignments available. Subjects covered in this chapter includes humanities, second languages, mathematics, and sciences. By the end of this chapter, the reader will be able to add and remove apps and extensions from the Chrome store and add-ons in Google Docs.

What you need for this book

In order to effectively utilize this book, you will need the following:

- A GAFE account. To attain this account, the school or educational institution that employs you must be part of the GAFE program. In order for students to access Google Classroom, they must also have a GAFE account. This book assumes that all core Google Apps such as Gmail, Google Calendar, Google Drive, and Google Docs are available, in addition to Google Classroom.
- A desktop or notebook computer connected to Internet running Windows Vista, Mac OS, or a Chromebook. The majority of instructions in this book are for desktop or notebook computers.
- Optionally, an Android or iOS mobile device.

Who this book is for

This book is for educators who want to use Google Classroom in their teaching practice. It is not just for geeks. There are rich examples, clear instructions, and enlightening explanations to help you put this platform to work, saving you valuable time. While this book is written in the high school perspective, it is applicable to teachers and educators of all age groups. If you are new to Google Classroom or a veteran who wants to learn more, this book will improve your online teaching capabilities.

Conventions

In this book, you will find a number of text styles that distinguish between different kinds of information. Here are some examples of these styles and an explanation of their meaning.

New terms and important words are shown in bold. Words that you see on the screen, for example, in menus or dialog boxes, appear in the text like this: "Click on **Create class** to create your first class:"

 Warnings or important notes appear in a box like this. Information that is found within these boxes emphasize important steps or provide additional information about the instructions or features.

Tips and tricks appear like this. Oftentimes, these will include anecdotal examples or events that I or other teachers have experienced while implementing Google Classroom in their classes.

Another convention that varies within this book is the use of first-person and third-person writing styles. Since this book is an instructional manual, much of the explanation and steps are in third person; however, teaching is highly individualistic. Therefore, information boxes, tips and tricks, and explanations may switch to first person to convey self-reflection on your unique circumstances. While GAFE includes the same core features, different schools and educational institutions choose which apps are available. Your teaching environment is most likely different from the author's, and these extra bits of information will help you adapt Google Classroom to your unique teaching style.

Reader feedback

Feedback from our readers is always welcome. Let us know what you think about this book—what you liked or disliked. Reader feedback is important for us as it helps us develop titles that you will really get the most out of.

To send us general feedback, simply e-mail feedback@packtpub.com, and mention the book's title in the subject of your message.

If there is a topic that you have expertise in and you are interested in either writing or contributing to a book, see our author guide at www.packtpub.com/authors.

Customer support

Now that you are the proud owner of a Packt book, we have a number of things to help you to get the most from your purchase.

Downloading the color images of this book

We also provide you with a PDF file that has color images of the screenshots/diagrams used in this book. The color images will help you better understand the changes in the output. You can download this file from https://www.packtpub.com/sites/default/files/downloads/TeachingwithGoogleClassroom_ColorImages.pdf.

Errata

Although we have taken every care to ensure the accuracy of our content, mistakes do happen. If you find a mistake in one of our books-maybe a mistake in the text or the code—we would be grateful if you could report this to us. By doing so, you can save other readers from frustration and help us improve subsequent versions of this book. If you find any errata, please report them by visiting http://www.packtpub.com/submit-errata, selecting your book, clicking on the **Errata Submission Form** link, and entering the details of your errata. Once your errata are verified, your submission will be accepted and the errata will be uploaded to our website or added to any list of existing errata under the Errata section of that title.

To view the previously submitted errata, go to https://www.packtpub.com/books/content/support and enter the name of the book in the search field. The required information will appear under the **Errata** section.

Piracy

Piracy of copyrighted material on the Internet is an ongoing problem across all media. At Packt, we take the protection of our copyright and licenses very seriously. If you come across any illegal copies of our works in any form on the Internet, please provide us with the location address or website name immediately so that we can pursue a remedy.

Please contact us at copyright@packtpub.com with a link to the suspected pirated material.

We appreciate your help in protecting our authors and our ability to bring you valuable content.

Questions

If you have a problem with any aspect of this book, you can contact us at questions@packtpub.com, and we will do our best to address the problem.

1
Getting to Know Google Classroom

Google Classroom is a **Learning Management System (LMS)** offered by Google to teachers. It provides a central location to communicate with students, pose questions, and create assignments. In an increasingly digital world, Google Classroom helps facilitate online learning for today's digital learners. Like many new applications, Google Classroom comes with a unique look and feel. Since your method of setting up your physical classroom is as unique as your method of teaching, Google Classroom begins as a blank canvas. Before we can add students into Google Classroom, you will need to create online classes for your physical classes. As you use Google Classroom, situations may arise where your class does not have a physical class associated with it. For example, distance learning classes and major school events may use Google Classroom without a physical class of students.

First, you will get comfortable with where everything is in Google Classroom. Being the teacher of the class will include options that are not visible to students and allow you to change settings such as what students can do in the Google Classroom. You will be able to add students to the class, create announcements and assignments, and upload course materials from this teacher view of the class. First, you will need to create and set up your class.

In this chapter, we will cover the following topics:

- Creating a class
- Changing the theme of a class
- Adding a title, description, and room location to the class
- Adding resources to the class such as files, YouTube videos, and websites
- Adding a co-teacher to the class

Creating your first Google class

To begin, open Google Chrome and navigate to `classroom.google.com`.

While Google Classroom is accessible from any web browser the Google Chrome web browser is built to be compatible with all of Google's other apps. Therefore, some features may be incompatible or will not function correctly in other web browsers. Consider discussing this with the IT department of your school if Google Chrome is not installed on your computer.

If this is the first time that you are accessing Google Classroom, the app will ask you whether to assign a teacher or student role to your account. Be sure to correctly select the teacher role, otherwise your account will be set as a student. You will not be able to create or manage classes unless your role is a teacher in Google Classroom.

If your account is set as a student account, you will need to contact your IT department so that they can change your Google Classroom role to a teacher:

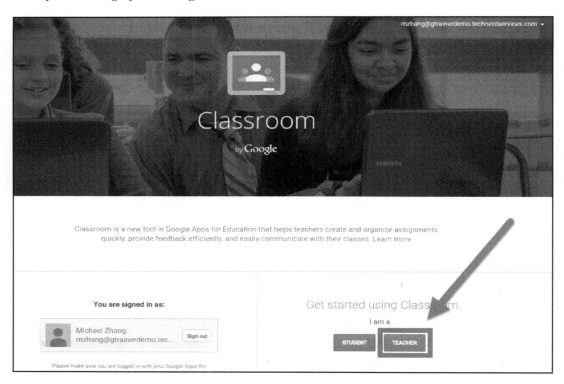

Another method of accessing Google Classroom is to use the App Launcher. If the IT department has enabled this feature, click on the waffle-shaped icon at the top-right corner of another Google app, such as Gmail, to see if the Google Classroom icon is available. The following is an example of the App Launcher:

Once you select the teacher role, the next page will point you towards a plus (**+**) symbol in the top-right corner to create your first class:

When you click on the plus symbol, a menu will appear for you to select whether to create a class or join a class. Click on **Create class** to create your first class:

As a teacher, you can join another teacher's class as a student by clicking on **Join class** and filling in the class code. These instructions are covered in detail in `Chapter 2`, *Inviting Students to Their Virtual Classroom*.

A dialog box will appear for you to name the class and provide a section number. While the class name is mandatory, the section number is optional. Depending on your school policies, specific classes may already have section numbers that you can add here. In Canada, many middle schools and high schools use section numbers for the timetable schedule, which is another option to fill in this field. Since students will also see the section number, using the timetable section number will be more applicable to students:

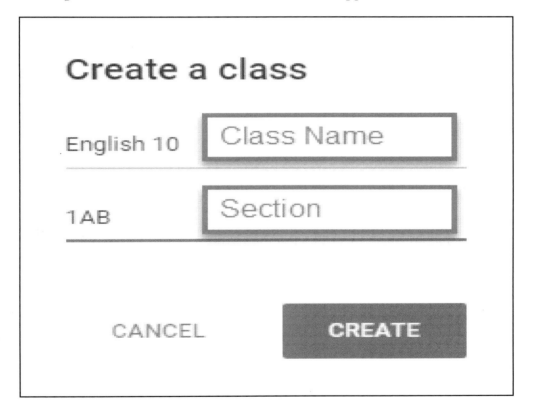

Once these fields are filled in and the **CREATE** button is clicked, you will be taken to your new class in Google Classroom:

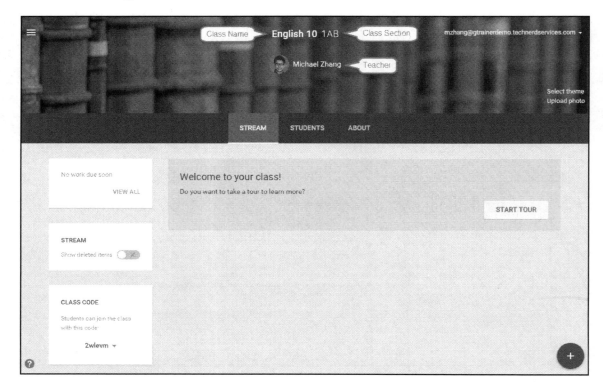

Navigating around Google Classroom

Now that your first class is set up in Google, you can see its different parts, the **Banner**, **Menu**, **Sidebar**, and **Content**:

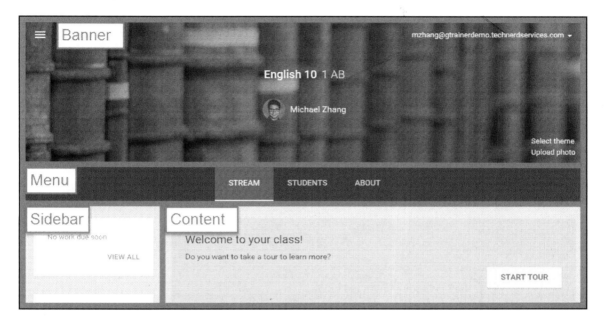

- **Banner** displays a banner image, class name, section, and teachers. The banner is the first thing students see when they enter the class, and it allows them to quickly identify which class they are accessing in Google Classroom.
- **Menu** allows teachers and students to switch between the different sections of Google Classroom. **Menu** has the following subsections:

    The **STREAM** page is where announcements, assignments, and discussion questions appear. The features within this section are elaborated in Chapter 3, *Sending Your First Announcement*; Chapter 4, *Starting an Online Discussion with Questions*; and Chapter 5, *Handing out and Taking in Assignments*.

    The **STUDENTS** page displays a list of all students enrolled in the class. Teachers can e-mail students from this section and change student-related settings in Google Classroom. The features of this section are elaborated in Chapter 2, *Inviting Students to Their Virtual Classroom*.

The **ABOUT** section displays the class title, description, and room number. Students are able to e-mail teachers from this section and find classroom material. Continue reading this chapter to learn about the features within the **ABOUT** section.

- **Sidebar** displays upcoming assignments, settings for the Stream, and the class code for students to be added to this class. The settings for the Stream and class code are only visible to the teacher.
- **Content** displays the current section in the class.

Personalizing the class theme

It's time to set up the class and start adding content. Similar to how teachers have a couple of days before students arrive at school to prepare their classroom, you need to take some time to add information to your online class before students are invited into the class. The tasks you can perform in Google Classroom are as follows:

- Changing the class theme
- Uploading a banner image
- Adding information about your class
- Adding files to your class

Changing the class theme

The class banner is the most prominent part of your class. It creates the atmosphere for the students when they arrive. Google Classroom will automatically apply a theme appropriate to the class name for common subjects. This feature is why the theme banner is books on a bookshelf for the English 10 class created in the previous section. The theme also changes the colors of the background and menus. To change your class theme, follow these steps:

1. Click on **Select theme** on the bottom-right corner of the banner image:

2. Select the desired Google Classroom provided banner image. The colors within the class will change to match the banner. Click on the **Select class theme** button:

Your class with the new theme will appear as shown in the following screenshot:

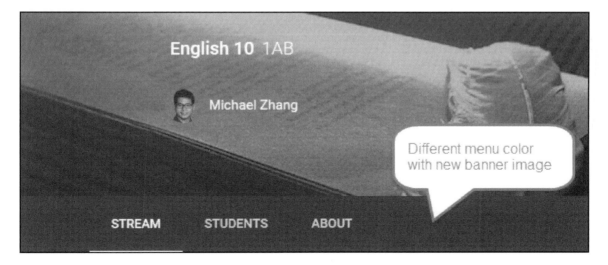

If this is your first foray into Google Classroom, try different themes before choosing one for your class. The most prominent colors in the banner image will suggest which colors the theme will use for the background and the menu.

Google Classroom also offers several patterns to use as the banner of the class. Simply select the **Patterns** tab in the dialog box to view the available patterns:

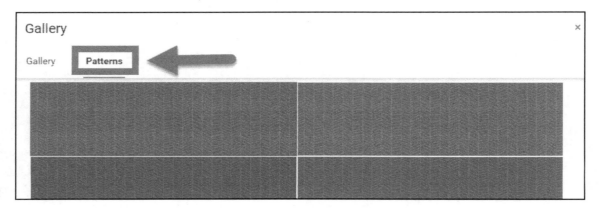

Uploading a banner image

Another alternative to using the images and patterns found within Google Classroom is to upload your own picture. The following steps will guide you through uploading a banner image.

1. Click on **Upload photo** at the bottom right corner of the banner image:

2. Click on the **Select a photo from your computer** button:

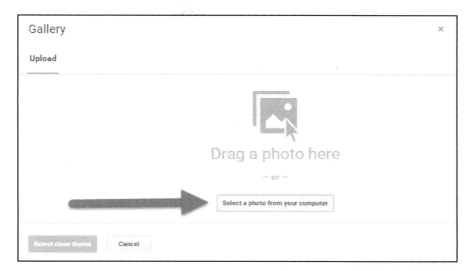

3. In the File Explorer, select the desired image and click on the **Open** button:

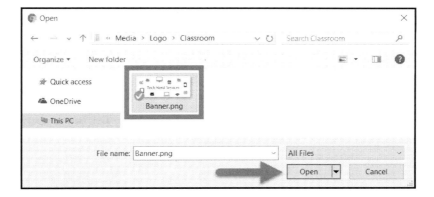

4. If the image is too large, crop the image by resizing the frame and move it to the desired location on the image.

Then click on the **Select class theme** button:

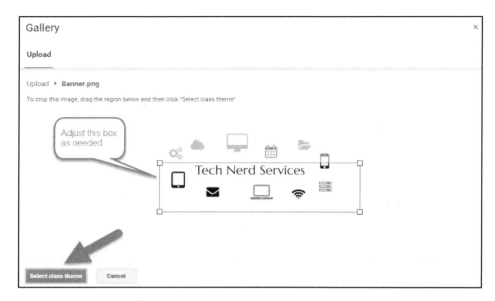

You will not be able to change the colors of the theme independently from those of the banner image.

Size matters when it comes to your banner image. Google Classroom will only use images with a pixel dimension of at least 800 x 200.

Once you have chosen the appropriate theme to personalize your Google class, you can start adding information and resources.

Adding information about your classroom

Students and co-teachers will be able to find information and resources related to the class in the **ABOUT** section of the Stream:

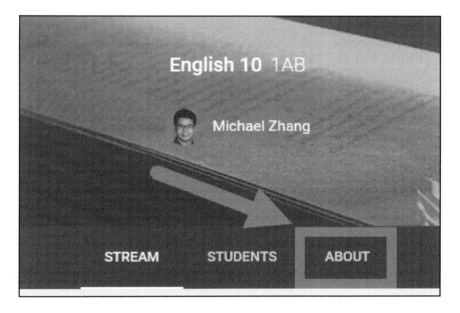

On your newly created site, the **Class Title**, **Class Description**, and **Room** fields will be blank. Filling in this information will provide students with a summary of what to expect from the class and where the physical room is, if your class also meets face-to-face. If you already have a course syllabus, filling in this section can be as easy as copying directly from your syllabus. The following screenshot shows where to enter the class information as well as links to the file folder in Google Drive and the class calendar in Google Calendar. Google Classroom automatically creates the folder in Google Drive during class creation, but does not create the calendar until the first assignment is posted in the Stream:

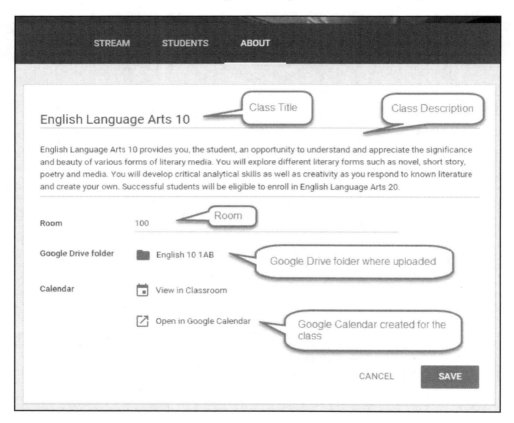

Once you have finished adding information about your class, you can also add files for your students to access.

Adding files to your classroom

There are two areas where you can add files to Google Classroom: The **STREAM** and the **ABOUT** page. Files uploaded to the **STREAM** page are for short term uses such as announcements or assignments, whereas files uploaded to the **ABOUT** page are relevant for the duration of the course, such as a course syllabus. Furthermore, you can use the **ABOUT** page to add files from Google Drive, link videos from YouTube, and link websites. In this section, you will upload a file from your computer to the **ABOUT** page, as follows:

1. In the **ABOUT** page, click on **Add materials…**:

2. In the **Title** field, give the resource a title.

3. Click on the paperclip icon:

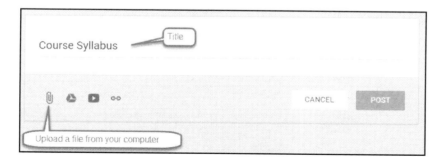

4. Click on the **Select files from your computer** button:

5. Find and open your file in File Explorer:

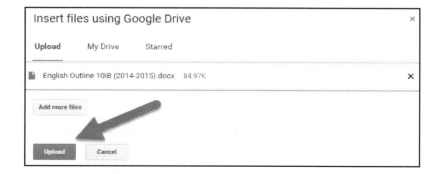

6. Click on the **Upload** button in the dialog box and watch your file upload:

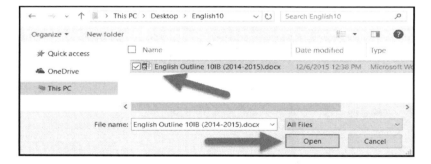

If you would like to add more files under the same title, simply click on the **Add more files** button to select another file to upload.

7. Click on the **POST** button to add the file to the **ABOUT** page:

Your file will now be available to students and co-teachers. The added material will display as a card on the **ABOUT** page. The uploaded files will be available in the Google Drive folder associated with the class:

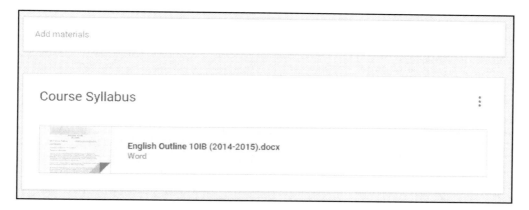

To add files from Google Drive, a YouTube video, or a website, click on the appropriate icon for each item. For YouTube videos and websites, you need the URL to add them to the **ABOUT** page:

Files added from Google Drive will remain in their locations within Google Drive instead of being moved to the folder associated with the class.

When you add materials to the **ABOUT** page, newer materials will appear closer to the top of the page. Therefore, plan which files you want to be readily accessible to your students when they appear on this page. If you want to reorder the cards, you can delete and recreate the cards in the desired order.

It is currently not possible to easily add Google Drive folders to Google Classroom. You can add all the files within a folder to the **ABOUT** page in a single card to mimic using a folder.

Storing files in Google Classroom

Whenever you upload files to Google Classroom, the files are stored in a folder in Google Drive. To view the contents of the folder, navigate to the **ABOUT** page of the class and click on the **Google Drive folder**:

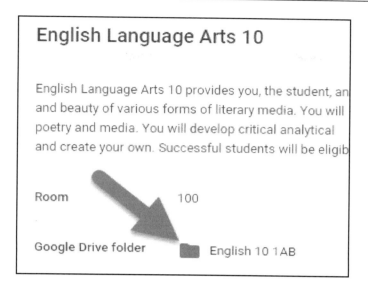

Uploaded files will appear in the Google Drive app:

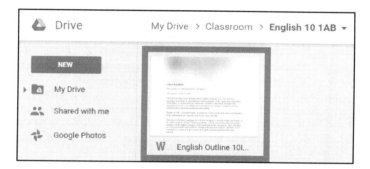

Inviting additional teachers

You might share teaching responsibilities with colleagues who also need access to the class on Google Classroom. By inviting other teachers, they will be able to do anything that you are able to do *except delete the class*.

Be sure that whoever you invite as a co-teacher is proficient with Google Classroom, because they can change and delete content, and there is no recorded history of what they do.

To invite another teacher to your class follow these steps:

1. In the **ABOUT** page, click on the **INVITE TEACHER** button in the sidebar:

2. Select the teacher from your **Contacts** and click on the **Next** button:

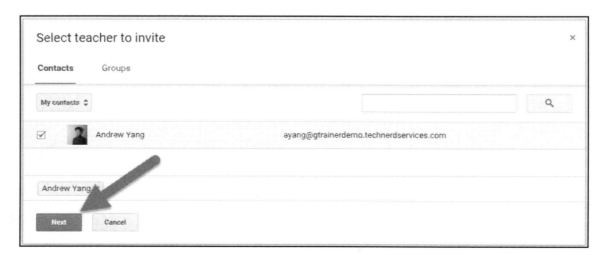

3. Confirm the invitation by clicking on the **INVITE** button:

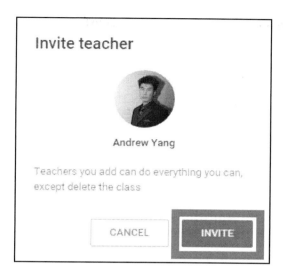

The invited teacher will appear grayed out in the sidebar until the teacher accepts the invitation. Once the co-teacher accepts the invitation, their name and image will also appear on the class banner:

Accessing classes from Google Classroom's homepage

Google Classroom's homepage displays all classes of which you are a teacher or student. The classes are arranged like cards on the page. The next time you go to Google Classroom, you will first arrive at the homepage, where you can select the desired class, as shown here:

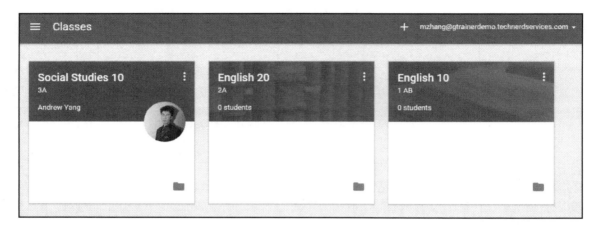

Classes in which you are enrolled as a student will have the image of the teacher on the class card.

Currently, you cannot rearrange the order in which the classes appear. Google Classroom arranges the classes in the order in which they were created.

When you are in a class, you can switch to a different class by clicking on the menu icon in the top- left corner of the banner:

The menu will appear from where you can select the desired class:

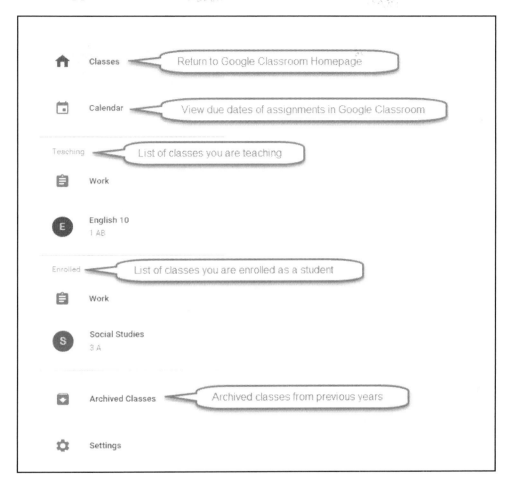

The menu is separated into the classes that you are teaching and the classes in which you are enrolled as a student. In addition, you can return to the Google Classroom homepage, view the Google Classroom calendar, access archived classes, and change the settings from this menu.

Summary

Your class is now online! In this chapter, you have personalized it, added information and materials, and invited a co-teacher.

After creating a class, you changed the theme of the class by using the various themes and patterns in Google Classroom. In addition, you uploaded a new image to use as a theme.

Then you added the class information in the About page, where you gave the class a title, description, and room number. Afterwards, you uploaded files to the About page. Finally, you invited another teacher to the class. These are the first steps towards accessing the time saving communication and management features of the app!

Now that the class is all set up, it's time to invite the students. In the next chapter, you will learn what it takes for students to access Google Classroom, as well as how to invite students to your class.

2
Inviting Students to Their Virtual Classroom

It's the start of the term and your physical and Google Classrooms are set up and ready for students to enter and for learning to commence. While students simply walk into your physical classroom, in your virtual classroom, students must join the class from a computer or a mobile device. As mentioned in the Preface, Google Classroom excels in classrooms where computers or mobile devices are readily available. Furthermore, students will use the tool more frequently if it is accessible on their own personal devices. If your school lends devices to students on a one-to-one basis, those devices may also need to be set up. Being the teacher, you may need to guide a class of students with different types of computers, tablets, and smart phones to install software and apps and set up Google Classroom. This chapter provides instructions for several types of devices. We will explore various methods of inviting students into a Google Classroom and managing those students within the class.

In this chapter, we will cover the following topics:

- Accessing Google Classroom on computers, Chromebooks, and mobile devices
- Using the class code to allow students to join the class
- Manually adding, removing, and e-mailing students within the class

Setting up Google Classroom on student devices

Like all of Google Apps, Google Classroom is accessible on any computer or mobile device connected to the Internet. However, not every student will access Google Classroom from the same type of device. Therefore, it is important that you can help guide your students in setting up Google Classroom.

The best time to invite students to Google Classroom is at the beginning of a term. During the first days of class, you will acclimatize your students to your classroom expectations and familiarize your students with the course syllabus. Setting up student devices can be easily integrated into this process so that students are ready to use Google Classroom at the start of the term, reducing the chance of technical difficulties later on.

Choosing the best time to invite students to Google Classroom
In general, I suggest that inviting students to Google Classroom and ensuring that all their devices are properly set up be done at the beginning of the term. However, this does not mean it has to be the first day. In Canadian high schools, students often have a couple of weeks to change their courses and thus change their timetable. Therefore, it may be more beneficial to wait until a majority of these changes are complete before inviting students to Google Classroom. It may save the number of manual changes you will have to make as the term progresses.

When students set up their devices, have them install the software or apps for Google Classroom on the device they will use most. If your school already has a computer lab, mobile laptop, or Chromebook cart that is not part of a one-to-one model, students will not need to set up those devices. For student populations with a high number of personal laptops, tablets, and smartphones, devoting class time to set up their personal devices will increase their use of Google Classroom.

The Google Classroom apps on iOS and Android provides push notifications to those devices. Therefore, encourage your students to set up the Google Classroom app on their smartphones so that they will always be notified whenever an announcement or assignment is posted in Google Classroom. Then you do not have to worry about students checking their school-issued e-mails for these Google Classroom notifications:

Computers and Chromebooks

Since Google Classroom and the rest of **Google Apps for Education** (**GAFE**) suite only require an Internet browser, laptops that run Microsoft Windows, Apple OS X, or Google's Chrome OS are all already able to access Google Classroom. While Microsoft Windows' default browser is Internet Explorer (or the new Microsoft Edge), and that of Apple OS X is Safari, Google develops and maintains its own Internet browser: Google Chrome. Using Google's Internet browser ensures the greatest compatibility with Google Classroom. Google Chromebooks already have Google Chrome installed; however, personal laptops used by students may not have Google Chrome installed.

 Chrome extensions are only compatible with Google Chrome. These are additional features added to Google Chrome that enhance Google Classroom. One example of a Chrome extension is Goobric, which Chapter 6, *Grading Written Assignments in a Flash*, explores.

Google's Chromebooks are the easiest to set up because they already have Google Chrome installed. Student profiles will automatically sync with the device when they first log in using their school credentials, regardless of whether it is a personal or school-issued Chromebook.

Google Chrome can be installed on a Windows and OS X computer with and without administrator privileges. Therefore, if a student does not have an administrator account on their personal device, the student can still install Google Chrome.

Installing Google Chrome in Microsoft Windows

To install Google Chrome on Microsoft Windows, follow these instructions:

1. Open another web browser, such as **Internet Explorer**:

2. In the address bar, navigate to `www.google.com/chrome`.

3. Hover your mouse over the **DOWNLOAD** menu and click on the **For personal computers** option:

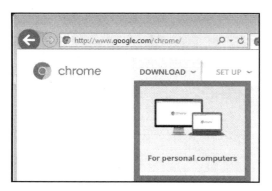

4. Click on the blue **Download Chrome** button in the center of the screen:

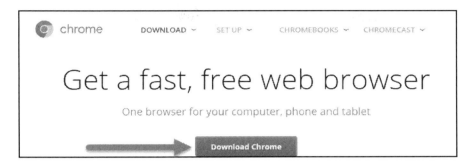

5. Accept **Google Chrome Terms of Service** by clicking on the blue **Accept and Install** button on the dialog box:

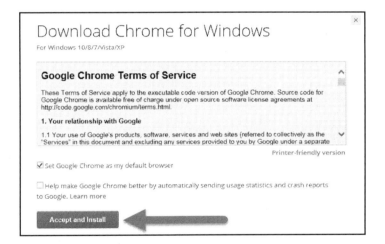

6. The computer will request permissions from an administrator's account. This section may ask for a password:

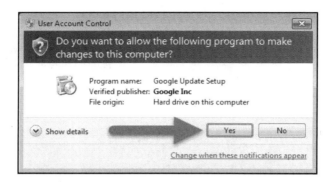

7. A dialog box will show the progress of downloading and installing Google Chrome:

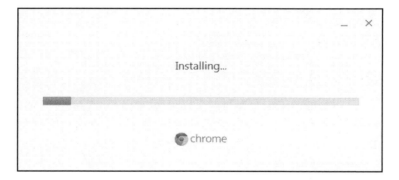

8. Once the installation is complete, Google Chrome can be launched from the shortcut on the desktop:

Installing Google Chrome on Apple OS X

Installing Google Chrome on Apple OS X is similar to installing it on Windows. The following instructions outline installing Google Chrome on OS X:

1. Open another web browser, such as **Safari**:

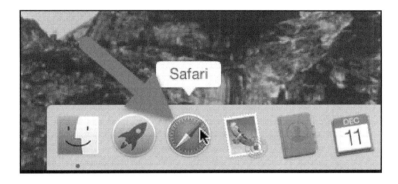

2. From the address bar, go to `www.google.com/chrome`:

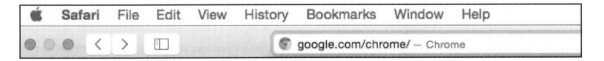

3. Hover your mouse over the **DOWNLOAD** menu and click on the **For personal computers** option:

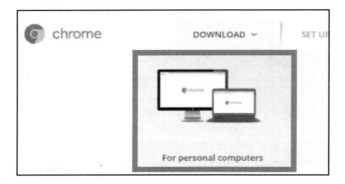

4. Click on the blue **Download Chrome** button in the center of the screen:

5. Accept **Google Chrome Terms of Service** by clicking on the blue **Accept and Install** button on the dialog box. A file will then be downloaded to the computer:

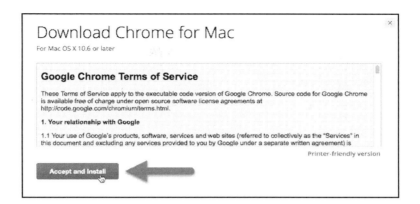

6. Double-click on the file that appears in the Dock. The file is named **googlechrome.dmg**:

7. Mac OS X will verify and open the program:

8. A dialog box will appear asking to copy Google Chrome into the **Applications** folder. Click and drag the Google Chrome icon into the **Applications** folder:

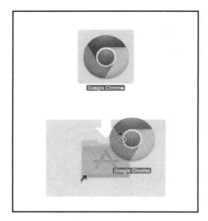

9. Google Chrome is now accessible from the **Applications** folder:

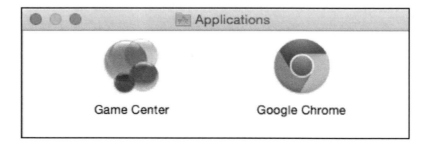

Installing Chrome without administrator permission

If the student does not have the password to the administrator's account, Google Chrome can still be installed on Mac OS X. However, the student will not be able to do step 8. Instead, the student can click and drag the Google Chrome icon to another location where the student's account has permission to save the files. One such location is the **Documents** folder in the student's account:

Adding a Google Chrome shortcut to the Dock

For quick access to Google Chrome, click and drag the Google Chrome icon from the **Applications** folder to the Dock:

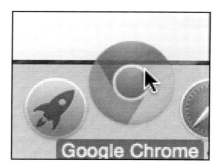

The first time the student launches Google Chrome, several dialog boxes will appear. These dialog boxes confirm opening a file downloaded from the Internet as well as ask whether the student wants to set Google Chrome as the default browser (the browser that opens whenever a link is clicked in another program).

Setting up Google Chrome

Once Google Chrome is installed, it must be linked to the student's account so that any bookmarks, Google Chrome apps and extensions will sync with their personal computer. To complete the set up with Google Chrome, complete the following steps:

1. Launch Google Chrome.
2. Click on the user icon at the top-right corner of Google Chrome:

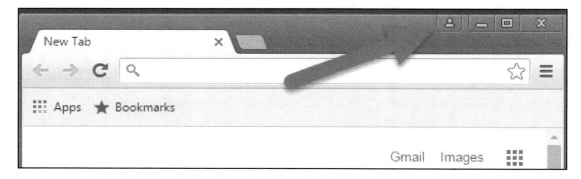

3. In the dialog box, click on **Sign in to Chrome**:

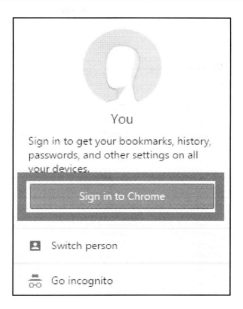

4. Enter the username and password, then click the **Sign in** button:

5. If Google Chrome displays another dialog box with the **Link your Chrome data to this account?** heading, click on the **Link data** button:

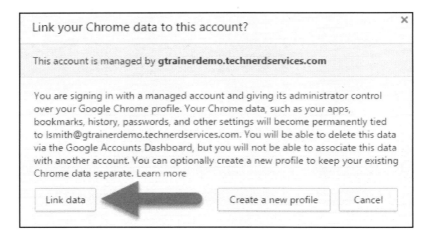

6. The user icon will now display the first name of the user:

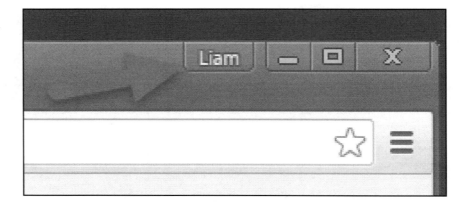

Tablets and phones

Many students may also need assistance in setting up Google Apps on their tablets and phones. Apart from downloading the apps from different app stores, installing Google Classroom is the same for Android and Apple iOS tablets and phones. For Google Classroom to function properly, additional Google Apps are required. The following steps outline installing Google Classroom on either Android or iOS:

1. Open the app store on the mobile device. For Android, the app store is called the **Play Store** and for iOS, it is **App Store**:

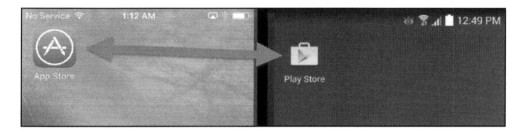

2. Tap the search icon at the bottom of the **App Store** in Apple iOS, or the search field at the top of the screen for Android, and search for Google Classroom:

3. Tap the **INSTALL** button beside the app. In iOS, you will need to tap **GET** and then **INSTALL**. Also, you may need to input the user's password:

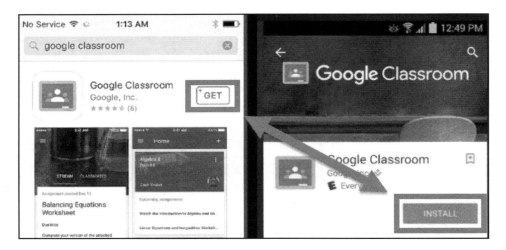

4. Tap the **OPEN** button to launch Google Classroom. When you need to launch the app in the future, find it on the Home screen in iOS and in the app drawer in Android:

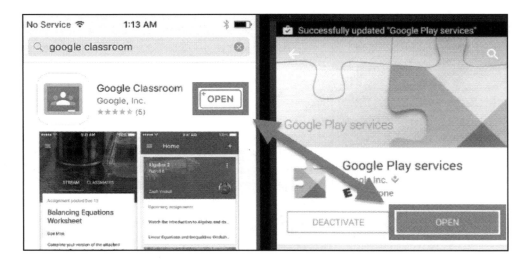

5. Click the **Add Account** or **Sign In** button:

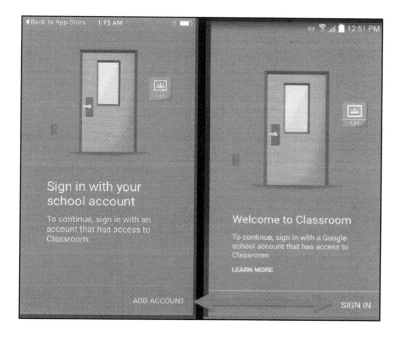

6. Enter the username and password and tap the **Sign in** button:

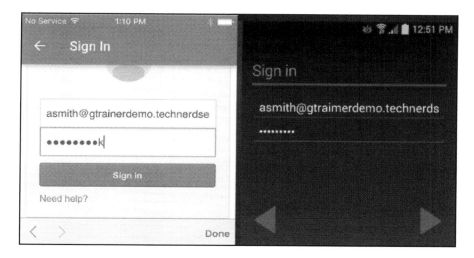

7. For iOS devices, there will be a pop-up asking whether Google Classroom can send notifications. Click on the **OK** button:

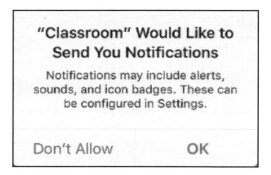

If another Google Account is already associated with the tablet or phone, click on the **Add account** option to enter the school-provided Google username and password:

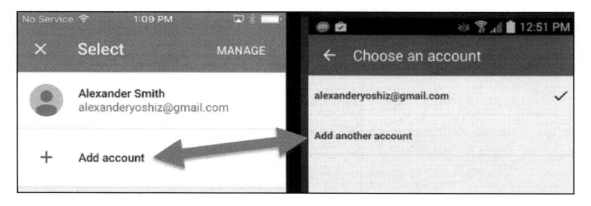

To use Google Classroom effectively, additional Google Apps also need to be installed on the mobile device. Simply follow the same steps to install the Google Classroom app. The following table lists the minimum apps that utilize features with Google Classroom:

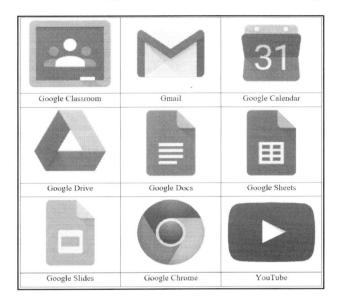

Google Classroom	Gmail	Google Calendar
Google Drive	Google Docs	Google Sheets
Google Slides	Google Chrome	YouTube

While these additional apps are not mandatory for the Google Classroom app to function, having students install them will reduce confusion later on. For example, if you create an assignment in Google Classroom with a Google Doc document attached, students who do not have the Google Docs app installed will not be able to open the file until they install the app. However, there may be features that your class does not need. If your students do not need to edit spreadsheets, then the Google Sheets app is unnecessary. As you use Google Classroom, modify this list to suit your content and activities.

 For Android devices, many of these additional apps are already installed on the tablet or phone.

Guiding students using the classroom projector

When guiding students through the installation of Google Classroom and adding Google Apps on mobile devices, connecting a mobile device to the classroom projector can help students through the installation process. Android devices may have built-in screen casting tools such as MHL or Miracast, whereas iOS devices can use an HDMI adapter to connect directly to a projector. If the projector does not have any of these features, Chromecast is a Google developed media streaming device that is compatible with newer Android devices. By connecting it to the projector's HDMI port, you can mirror an Android device's screen on the projector. An alternative to connecting the mobile device directly to the projector is placing the tablet or phone on a document camera. Middle and high school students most likely already have experience in installing apps on their mobile devices. Therefore, displaying which apps are needed on the projector is most likely all that is required to ensure that the students install all the apps.

Allowing students to join using the class code

Now that the students have the appropriate apps to use Google Classroom on their computers and mobile devices, it is time for your students to join your class in Google Classroom. Students can join specific classes in Google Classroom using the class code. This is a combination of letters and numbers that identify the unique class in Google Classroom. Any student with a school-issued Google e-mail can join your class if they have access to the class code.

 A student can use any device to join a class. Furthermore, once the student has joined your class on a device, they will be able to access your class from any other device where they log in with their school e-mail.

Joining a classroom with the class code

Use the following steps to guide students to join your classroom:

1. On a laptop or Chromebook, open Google Chrome and from the address bar, navigate to `classroom.google.com`. On a tablet or smartphone, tap the Google Classroom app:

2. Click or tap on **+** at the top-right of the page:

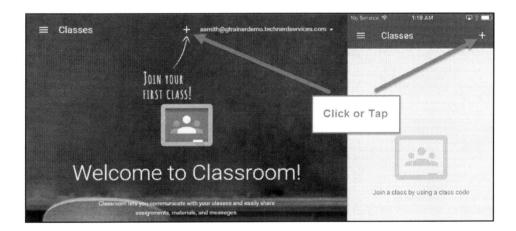

3. Enter the class code provided by the teacher. Then click on the **JOIN** button:

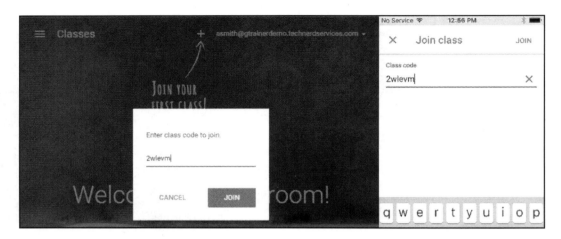

The students will immediately enter your Google Classroom class and the class will appear on the Home page of their Google Classroom app, as shown in the following screenshot:

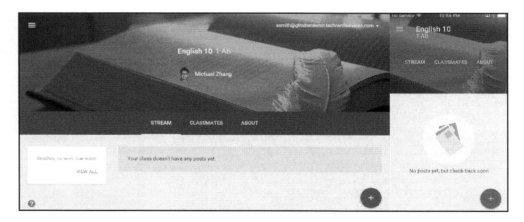

Displaying the class codes in your physical classroom
At the beginning of the term, display your class codes in your classroom so that students who are added to your class later can easily join. A corner of a whiteboard or bulletin board is an excellent location.

Making changes to the class code

After all your students have joined your classes, you can prevent other students from joining your classes by either resetting the class code or disabling it altogether. Resetting the class code will generate a new code for students to use to join your classroom. Apart from resetting the class code, teachers cannot customize the class code. This change will not affect the students already within your class. Disabling the class code will prevent students from joining the class; however, you will still be able to manually invite students. To reset or disable the class code, follow these instructions:

1. In the Stream of your class, click on the code in the **CLASS CODE** box in the sidebar:

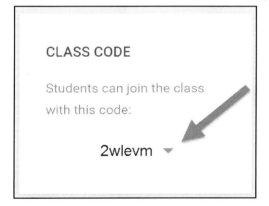

2. From the drop-down menu, either select **Reset** or **Disable**:

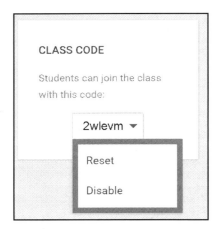

The class code can also be changed in the options found at the top of the **STUDENTS** section.

The class code is a setting that is available on the mobile apps. It is found in the menu of the **STUDENTS** section:

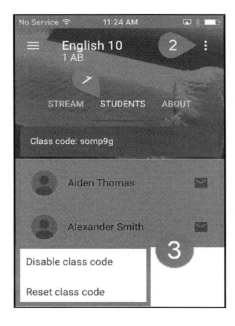

Managing students in your classroom

The full class list of all students can be found in the **STUDENTS** section of your class. You will be able to make changes to the students within your class as well as send e-mails to individual students or to the entire class.

Manually inviting students to your classroom

When students are added to your class late in the term or a student is having difficulties joining with the class code, you can manually invite students to your classes. You should use this method as a last resort because manually adding several dozen students to a class is tedious and time-consuming. Follow these instructions to manually invite a student to your class:

While writing this book, mobile devices were unable to add or remove students from the class. It was still possible to send e-mails to individual students from the mobile app.

1. In Google Classroom, click on the **STUDENTS** section in the menu and then click on the **INVITE** button:

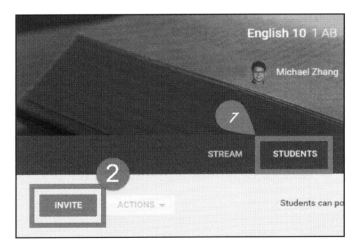

2. The dialog box will show **My Contacts** by default. Use the drop-down menu to change the view to **Directory**:

The Directory is the shared contacts across the school district. The district IT must enable this feature. Otherwise, you will need to save the students school e-mail as a contact before you will be able to select it here.

3. Search for your student with the search field or scroll down the student list and select the student. Click the **Invite Students** button when all desired students are selected:

Once a student is invited, the student will appear grayed out until the student accepts the invite:

The student will need to accept the invitation by logging into Google Classroom from a computer/Chromebook (left) or on a mobile device (right) and clicking or tapping on the **JOIN** button:

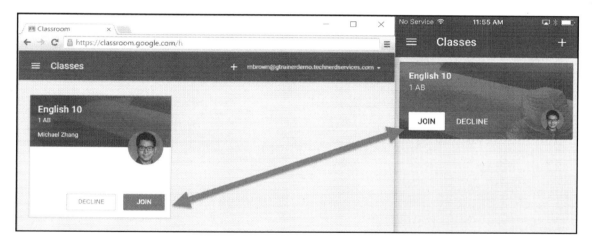

Another rare situation where you may need to manually invite a student to your class is if the student unenrolls from the class. Students are able to unenroll themselves from a class from the Home screen of Google Classroom. At the time of writing, there is no way to disable this feature for students:

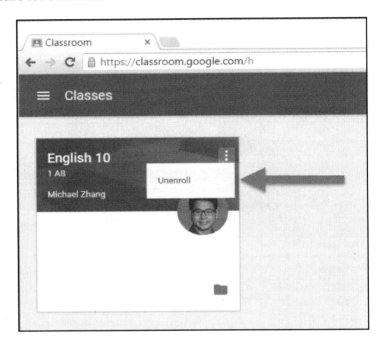

Removing students from your classroom

When students withdraw from your physical class, you will also need to remove them from your class in Google Classroom. Removing a student from your Google class is the same as the student unenrolling. While not mandatory, the withdrawn student will still receive announcements and assignments through Google Classroom if they are still enrolled in your class. The following steps will remove a student:

1. In Google Classroom, click on the **STUDENTS** section:

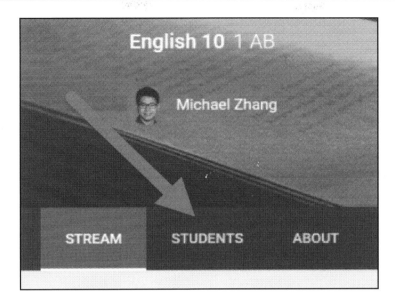

2. Click on the checkbox beside the student. (You can also select additional students if you need to remove multiple students.) Then click on the **ACTIONS** drop–down menu:

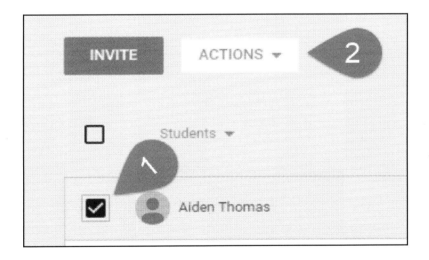

3. Select the **Remove** option:

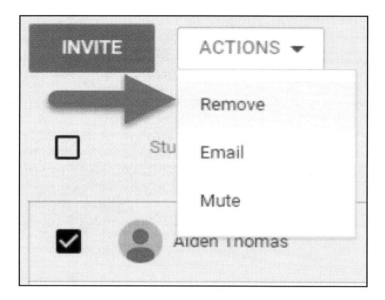

Emailing students in your classroom

When you need to communicate with an individual or a small group of students, you can send an e-mail directly from Google Classroom. However, Google Classroom has an Announcement feature when you need to communicate with the entire class. This Announcement feature is discussed in Chapter 3, *Sending Your First Announcement*. To e-mail students from Google Classroom, follow the steps given in the previous section. Instead of selecting **Remove**, select **Email**, and a new e-mail message window will appear addressed to the selected students.

Summary

If this is the first time that you are inviting students to your virtual classroom, the steps in this chapter may appear daunting. However, through past experience, today's middle and high school students already have a proficient understanding of technology and will complete these tasks quickly. When I was teaching with Google Classroom, the setup process only took about fifteen minutes with high school students. This chapter gives you the tools for those students who have never used Google Classroom, which, as years go by, will decrease.

You are now able to install Google Chrome on Windows or Apple computers, as well as guide students through the installation of Google Classroom and other Google Apps on their mobile devices. You can display the class code to allow students to join your classes as well as manually invite or remove students as needed. Finally, you are able to e-mail students directly from Google Classroom.

This chapter recommended that you e-mail students only individually or in small groups. In the next chapter, you will explore how to use the Announcement feature to communicate with your entire class.

3
Sending Your First Announcement

Now that your online class is set up in Google Classroom and your students are enrolled in their classes, you can begin using Google Classroom features to communicate with the students. One of the simplest forms of communicating with students within your class is to send announcements. Announcements in Google Classroom are similar to sending your class an e-mail. (In fact, when you create an announcement, students also receive an e-mail with the information.) For announcements, you can add files from your computer or Google Drive and add links to websites or YouTube videos. Students can even reply to your announcements directly from the classroom Stream. An announcement is a type of post that appears in the Stream and shares many features also found in the Question and Assignment posts. Using announcements in Google Classroom instead of sending e-mails also makes it easier to find announcements in the future and use them in other classes.

In this chapter, we will cover the following topics:

- Sending and receiving announcements
- Parts of an announcement
- Replying to announcements
- Editing announcements
- Reusing announcements
- Authorizing and managing students in the Stream

Creating an announcement

An announcement appears at the top of the classroom Stream. Whenever new posts, such as an announcement, question, or assignment, are added to the Stream, the post will be added to the top of the Stream. Therefore, older posts in the Stream are moved lower down the Stream.

 New announcements are added to the top of the Stream. Older posts in the Stream move lower in the Stream, but are not deleted.

To create an announcement, go to the desired class and follow the following directions:

1. In the Stream, click on the **+** icon at the bottom-right of the page.
2. Select the message bubble icon titled **Create announcement**:

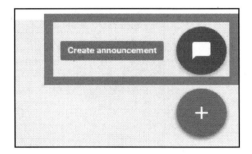

3. Type your announcement in the field:

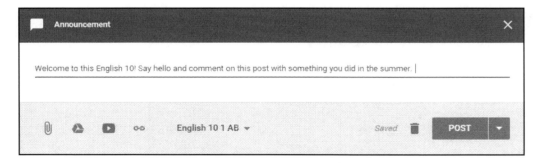

4. If you would like to post this announcement in multiple classes at the same time, click on the name of the class to select additional classes:

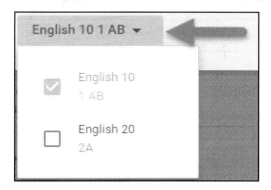

5. Click the **POST** button when you are ready to post:

If you are not ready to post the announcement, you can save it as a draft by clicking on the drop-down menu beside the **POST** button and selecting **Save draft:**

Google Classroom places drafts at the top of the Stream:

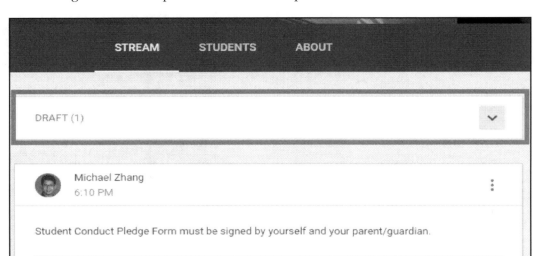

Scheduling a time to publish an announcement

As of May 2016, teachers can schedule when Google Classroom will publish a post. This feature allows you to set up announcements, questions, assignments, or quizzes, and post them at appropriate times during the lesson. A simple example of utilizing this feature is posting a Question post as a *Do Now* at the start of class, followed by another Question or Assignment post halfway through the lesson to assess student's understanding, and ending the lesson with an Assignment post with practice questions. To schedule a post, in the drop-down menu of the **POST** button, select **Schedule**, as shown here:

The following dialog box shows how to set the date and time when Google Classroom will publish the post. Clicking on the **SCHEDULE** button confirms the publishing time and saves the post:

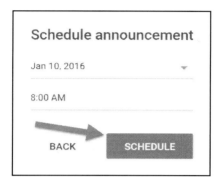

Just like drafts, scheduled posts appear in a collapsed section above the Stream.

Advanced features in announcements

Announcements can communicate more than a simple text message. Some additional features of an announcement include:

- Attaching a file from your computer
- Attaching a file from Google Drive
- Including a YouTube video
- Including a link to a website

When to add resources to the Stream or to the About sections

You may have already noticed that these options are also present in the About section described in Chapter 1, *Getting to Know Google Classroom*. Adding files to specific posts instead of to the About section indicates that the included resources are for the specific post in the Stream instead of the class in general. Posts will move lower down the Stream faster than they will in the About section. Therefore, resources attached in the Stream are for short-term tasks, whereas resources attached in the About section are for the duration of the class.

The following screenshot shows where many of these features are present in the **Announcement** dialog box when creating an announcement:

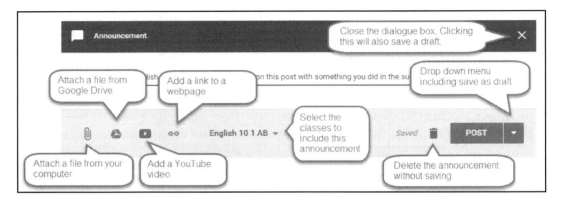

Attaching a file from your computer

When you attach a file from your computer to a post, the file will be available to the students when they view the announcement. Here are the steps to attach a file from your computer when creating an announcement:

1. Click on the paperclip (📎) icon in the **Announcement** dialog box.
2. Click on the **Select files from your computer** button in the dialog box:

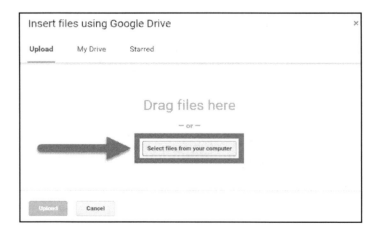

3. Navigate to the desired file and click the **Open** button:

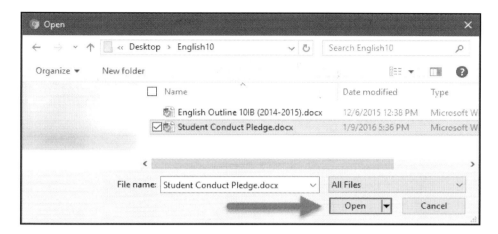

4. Click on the **Upload** button:

To add multiple files, click on the **Add more files** button to open the File Explorer and add additional files before clicking on the **Upload** button.

5. Click on the **POST** button of the create **Announcement** dialog box:

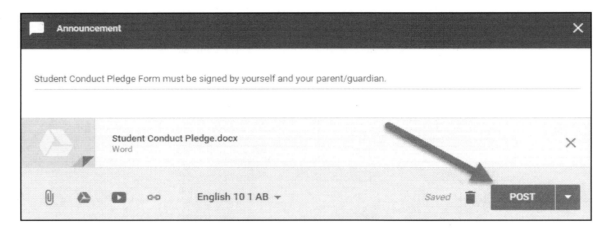

Files that are uploaded are stored in the Classroom folder in Google Drive, just like the files that are uploaded in the resources section on the About page.

Attaching a file from Google Drive

Attaching a file from Google Drive is similar to attaching a file from your computer. The steps are as follows:

1. Click on the Google drive ( ) icon in the **Announcement** dialog box.

2. Navigate to the desired file in Google Drive. Select the file and then click the **Add** button:

3. Click on the **POST** button of the create **Announcement** dialog box:

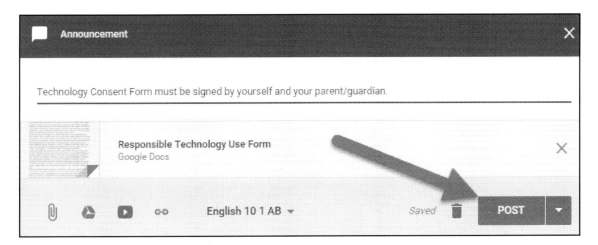

Including a YouTube video

The YouTube dialog box that appears when the YouTube icon is clicked allows you to search, and add a specific video:

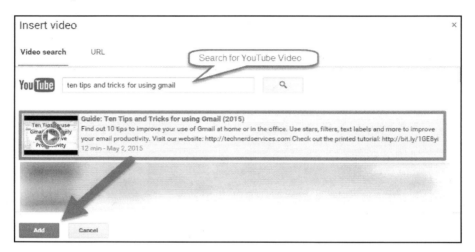

If you have already saved the video on YouTube, another method is to copy the YouTube address and paste it into the field of the URL tab:

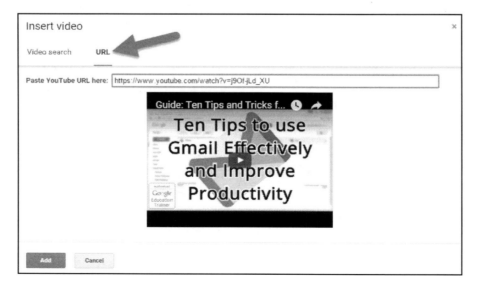

Including video files in a post

At first glance, Google Classroom does not appear to play videos already saved to your computer. However, Google Drive uses a built-in video player similar to YouTube. Therefore, you can attach a video file to the post and students will be able to watch the video. Google Drive has a five terabyte file size limit and can play WebM, MPEG-4, MP4, 3GPP, MOV, AVI, MPEG-PS, WMV, FLV, and MTS video files.

Making changes to an announcement in the Stream

You may need to make changes or outright delete an announcement or another type of post after the post is already published on the Stream. Each post has a vertical line of three dots to indicate a menu of actions that can be performed on the post:

In the menu, you will be able to perform the following actions on the announcement (or any other type of post) in the Stream:

- **Move to top**: This will place the announcement at the top of the Stream.
- **Edit**: This will allow you to make changes to the announcement.
- **Delete**: This will remove the post and all comments and attachments associated with the post from the Stream.
- **Copy Link**: This will copy the direct link to the post. This link can then be pasted into another method of communication, such as an e-mail.

Teachers and co-teachers can Move to top, edit, and delete each other's posts.

Emphasizing specific posts with Move to top
Keeping specific posts at the top of the Stream will help remind students of important announcements. These announcements may include reminders for school-wide events, deadlines, and field trip forms.

Reusing a previously created announcement

All your classes may not be learning at the same pace. Therefore, you may have a class that needs the same post as a faster-paced class. Instead of retyping or copying and pasting the information, Google Classroom provides a feature to copy an entire post from one class and repost it in another class. Follow these steps to reuse a post:

1. In the class that you wish to repost the previous announcement, click on the + icon and select the **Reuse post** action:

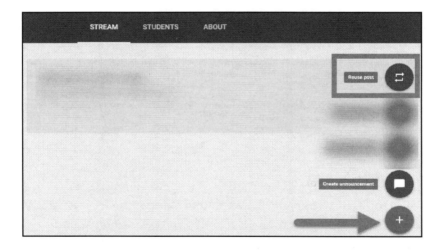

2. Select the class that has the previously created post and click the **SELECT** button:

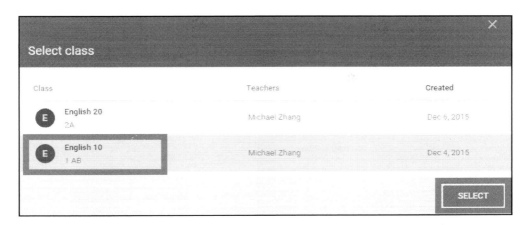

3. Select the desired post and click the **REUSE** button. Attachments are copied to the new post by default:

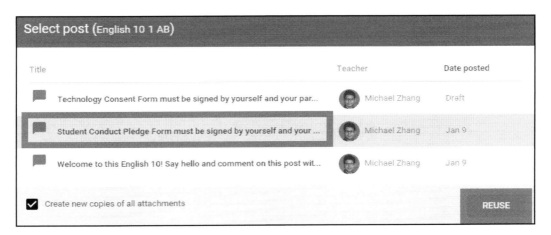

4. The create **Announcement** dialog box will appear with all the information filled from the previous post. You can make changes before posting the announcement in the new class:

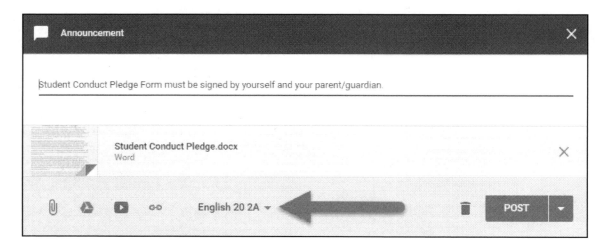

How students receive announcements

By default, students will receive e-mail notifications when you post an announcement (or any other type of post) on the Stream:

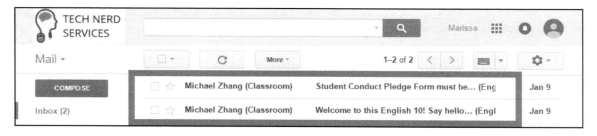

These e-mails contain the title and link to the post in Google Classroom. Another method whereby students receive notifications is through the Google Classroom app on their smart device:

Disabling e–mail notifications

If you or your students do not wish to receive e-mail notifications whenever a co-teacher or student posts in the Stream, you can disable e-mail notifications from within Google Classroom. Here are the steps:

1. In Google Classroom, click on the menu (▤) button in the classes banner.
2. Scroll to the bottom of the menu and click on the settings (⚙) icon.
3. Uncheck **Send email notifications**:

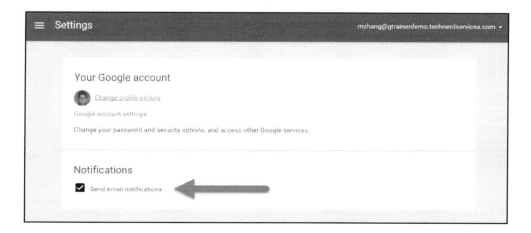

Another method to get to the settings screen is to click on the link found at the bottom of an e-mail notification, as shown in the following screenshot:

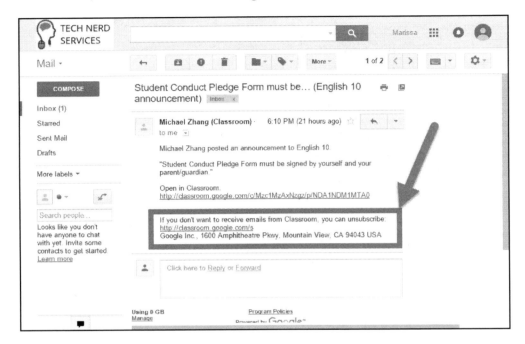

Commenting on announcements

Once posts are published in the Stream, students and co-teachers will be able to comment on the announcements. These comments promote discussion and are similar to having students ask questions after giving a verbal announcement during class time. Furthermore, in other types of posts, such as Questions and Assignments, students can use this commenting feature to reply to specific questions within the post.

For students to comment on a post, direct them to follow these steps:

1. In the classroom's Stream, click on the **Add class comment...** row at the bottom of the post:

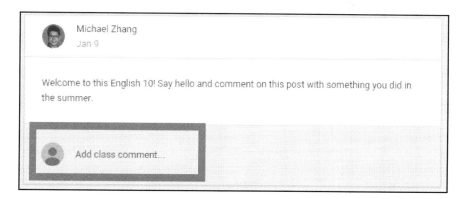

2. A field will appear for the student to enter text. Direct the students to click the **POST** button when they are done entering their comment.

Comments on a post are displayed for everyone in the class. Inappropriate use of the commenting feature in Google Classroom can detract from the learning environment. Later in this chapter, you will learn how to manage students who abuse the commenting system.

As shown in the following screenshot, it does not take long for students to comment on a post in the Stream. Students will often respond to other student comments and guide a discussion without too much additional input from the teacher:

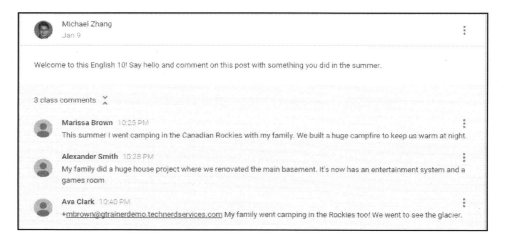

 Using online discussions can be a great method for shy or quiet students to have an alternative environment where they may feel safer to communicate.

Replying to comments

As more students and teachers comment on posts, individuals can comment on specific posts. Replying to a specific comment on a post automatically adds that user as a mention. However, the comment appears at the bottom of the thread instead of directly below the comment that is replied to:

To reply to a comment, click on the reply (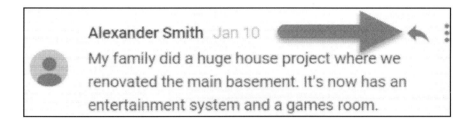) icon that appears when hovering the mouse over the comment. Then continue writing your comment as normal:

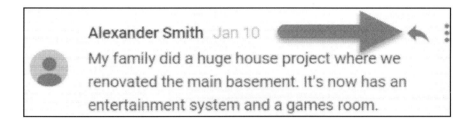

Managing comments

Since comments are published immediately, student comments may need managing and monitoring. There are several tools to help teachers control which students can comment.

Editing and deleting comments

Teachers and the comment's creator can edit and delete a comment. Deleted comments are immediately removed from the Stream, but as a teacher, you will be able to view deleted comments and posts. To edit or delete a comment, click on the three vertical dots to display a menu with the actions:

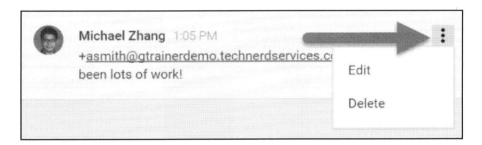

You cannot edit a student's comment, but can only delete their comment. If there are replies to a comment, they will remain as comments to the post.

If you need to view deleted posts and comments in the Stream, click on the switch titled **Show deleted items** in the sidebar:

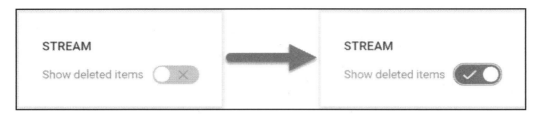

Muting students

If there is a student that is particularly inappropriate on the Stream, you can disable that student's ability to reply to another classmate's work, post, or comment in the Stream. To mute or unmute a student, click on the three vertical dots menu of the comment to display the menu with the mute action:

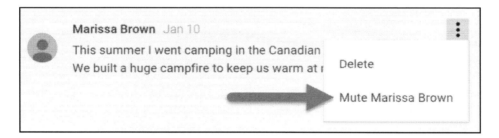

In the Stream and in the student list, a mute () icon will be displayed beside the student's name so that you can easily see which students are muted.

If a student is muted within a class, other classmates will not be able to see the mute icon beside their name. Only teachers and co-teachers will be able to see this icon.

Another method for muting students is in the **STUDENTS** section. This method also allows you to mute or unmute multiple students at once. To use this method, follow these steps:

1. In Google Classroom, navigate to the **STUDENTS** section using the menu:

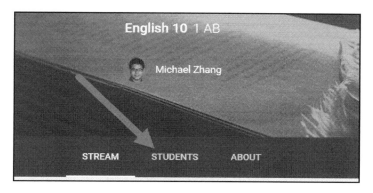

2. Check the checkboxes beside the students that you will mute (or unmute):

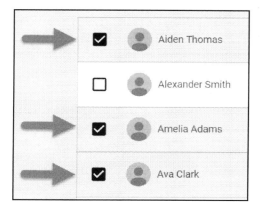

3. Click on the **ACTIONS** menu at the top of the student list and select **Mute** (or Unmute):

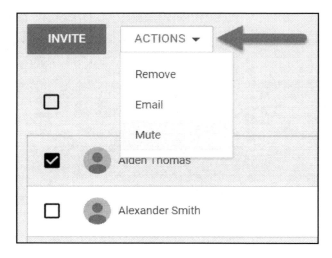

Viewing all muted students at a glance

You can see the mute icon beside all student names in the class list. Therefore, finding muted students in this list is easier than finding the muted student in the Stream:

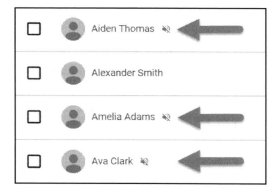

 Muting students may hinder class discussion on the Stream. An alternative to use the comment feature is to post a Question, which will be discussed in Chapter 4, *Starting an Online Discussion with Questions*.

Disabling comments in the Stream

Despite all the comment-managing features in Google Classroom, you may decide that your class is not ready for this feature or you prefer that students do not comment in the Stream. It is possible to completely disable the commenting feature using the following steps:

1. In Google Classroom, navigate to the **STUDENTS** section using the menu:

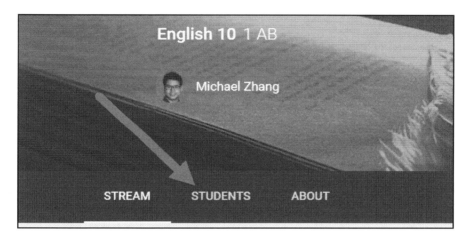

2. At the top of the class list, click on the **Students can post and comment** to display a menu of different options for student access to the Stream:

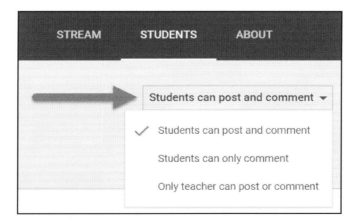

You can change the level of student access to the Stream at any time. As a means of classroom management, you can enable comments temporarily and then disable them (or vice versa) depending on your needs and the behavior of your students.

Summary

This chapter provided you with a foundation to post on the class Stream. While we only discussed the Announcement post, many of the features found in the Announcement post, such as attaching files, links, and YouTube videos, is available for all the other post types. As you continue to use Google Classroom, the Stream will become a central location for you and your students to view most announcements, assignments, and discussions, which saves time in organization and assessment.

You are now able to create an Announcement post in Google Classroom, attach resources to the post, and reuse posts in other classes. In addition, you can comment on posts and manage student comments by deleting individual comments, muting students, or disabling the comment feature entirely.

For situations where you disable comments, or as another means of interacting with your students, the next chapter will discuss the additional features found in the Question post type.

4
Starting an Online Discussion with Questions

The Stream has many different types of posts available for teachers. Each type of post has a different set of features that allow teachers to communicate differently with students. While the previous chapter discussed announcements and how students can comment on announcements, you may have situations where you want to record who responded to a post and even grade that response. An example of this situation is when you want to have a dialogue similar to a classroom discussion, but through Google Classroom.

There are several advantages of having discussions through Google Classroom. In a generation of instant messaging and texting, many students will feel comfortable dialoguing through an online tool. Furthermore, students do not have to be in the same location to participate. During my time teaching, there were times when students were absent on critical discussion days and could not be assessed. In addition, students are able to take time to formulate their responses, rather than being put on the spot during a discussion. Therefore, students tend to feel more secure discussing online instead of in a class because of familiarity and a decreased chance of failure.

Online or offline discussions

There is a delicate balance between the use of online and in-class discussions. Favoring one form of discussion can reduce the effectiveness of the other. Consider incorporating both types of discussion. Some examples of methods of incorporating both online and in-class discussion include asking a discussion question online and then asking follow up questions in class the next day, or discussing different topics in class and online.

A use of Question posts is to quickly check student understanding. In Alberta, teachers use formative assessment to gauge whether students comprehend the current concept before moving to the next concept. Since Question posts allow students to respond in short sentences or answer multiple choice questions, a question in Google Classroom can show you if the majority of your students understand the current lesson.

In this chapter, you will learn how to create short answer and multiple choice questions using the Question post in the classroom Stream, reply to, and grade the student responses.

 Google Classroom calls a student's response to a Question post an *answer*. However, because of the teaching philosophy of the author, this chapter will refer to them as *responses*.

Creating a question

With the different types of posts within the Stream, many of the features, such as attaching a file, use the same steps as the Announcement post. However, posts such as the Question and Assignment posts have additional features. If you are reading this book out of the chapter order, refer to the previous chapter, *Sending Your First Announcement* for the features that are also found in announcements.

Create questions in the Stream by selecting the **Create Question** icon in the + icon, as shown in the following screenshot:

Additional features in the Question post not found in the Announcement post

The following screenshot is the dialog box that appears when creating a Question post:

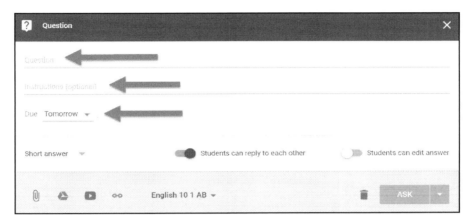

There are three fields in a Question post, whereas an Announcement post has only one. Furthermore, the Question post has questions options that affect the type of question and how students interact with each other within the question:

- **Question**: This field is where you write your question. It only allows you to include text without formatting. (If you need to include an image with your question, you can use the attach feature.)
- **Instructions**: This field is where you can write additional steps or expectations of the question. For example, you may want to instruct students that they must also reply to another student's response.
- **Due**: This field allows you to assign when students must have their responses submitted. This field includes the option to select a specific time and date.

Questions (and assignments) do not require a due date. Within the drop-down menu for due date and time, click on the **X** beside the date to disable the due date:

While not necessary, having due dates on questions and assignments will add the events to the Google Calendar linked to the Google Classroom. In Chapter 8, *Keeping Parents in the Loop*, you will learn how to allow parents to view the calendar.

The question options, found below the due date, depend on the question type: short answer and multiple choice. Each subsequent section will explore these options.

Creating short answer questions

The short answer question type is the default question type. Depending on how the question options are set, the short answer question type can perform two different tasks: student collaboration or teacher assessment. The **students can reply to each other** question option allows the teacher to determine whether students can see and reply to the responses of other classmates. By disabling this option, only the teacher (and co-teachers) will be able to see the responses and assess each student's response individually. However, by leaving this option enabled, students can reply to each other's responses, encouraging student collaboration through online discussion.

The second option for short answers, is **students can edit answer**. By enabling this option, students will be able to edit their responses after their submission. By leaving this option disabled, the following warning prompt will appear before confirming the student's submission:

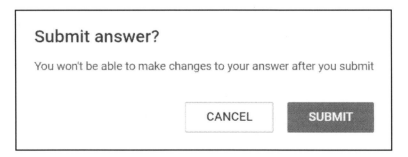

When to allow student edits

Generally, it is better to leave this option disabled. Preventing students from altering their submission is not available in the Assignment post discussed in the next chapter. Even when they are unable to edit their submission, students are able to add private comments to their response. In online collaboration, a student is able to reply to their own response. Therefore, using private comments and replies leaves the response unaltered in case it needs to be referenced in the future.

Once all the necessary fields are filled and the appropriate question options are set, click on the **ASK** button to post the question, as shown here:

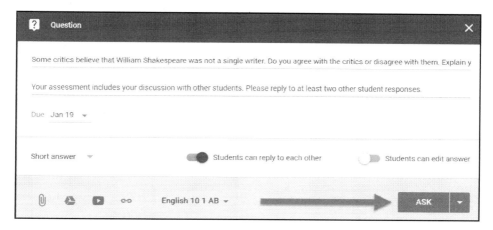

Questions in the Stream appear with a question mark icon, and you will be able to see how many students have answered the question as well as when the question is due. This is shown in the following screenshot:

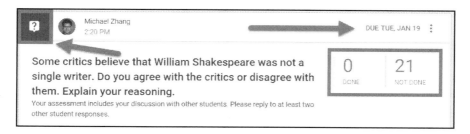

Making changes to a Question post, such as editing and deleting, works the same as in an Announcement post. Refer to the previous chapter, *Sending your First Announcement* for the steps.

The student view

Students will see the question differently on the Stream. They will only see the question, be able to respond to the question, and submit their response directly on the post:

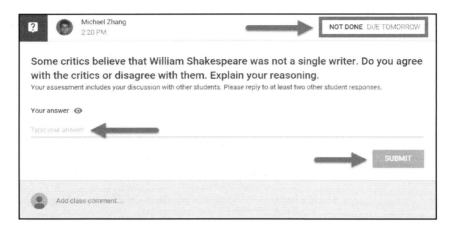

Once the student's answer is submitted, if the question option is enabled, they will be able to see how many other students have replied to their response as well as view other student's responses:

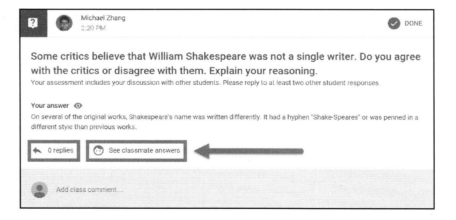

Google Classroom utilizes several Google Apps to communicate with the student. Not only does Google Classroom send an e-mail, because this question has a due date, it will also create an event on the due date to remind the student in Google Calendar. Furthermore, when the student goes to the class in Google Classroom, the first box in the sidebar, shown in the following screenshot, will list the question:

Students are still able to submit responses after the due date. The Question post in the Stream will show a **LATE** indicator at the top of the post, as shown:

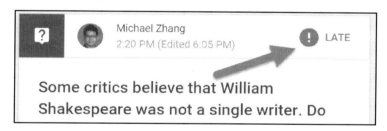

Once the response is submitted, the post will indicate that the question was responded to late:

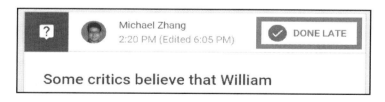

Replying to student responses

Teachers and students can reply to student responses. Replying to a response is not the same as commenting on a post in the Stream. Commenting on the Question post is about the content of the question. For example, a student may comment on the question if the due date can be extended. Replying to a response is only about the individual response. While students can use the **See classmate answers** link in the Question post after they submit their response, the following steps outline a method that teachers or students can use to find student answers and reply to them:

1. In the classroom Stream, click on the title of the question. The next page will show all student responses:

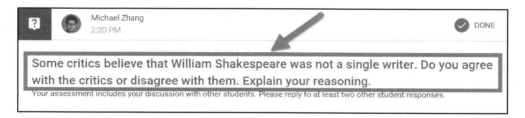

2. To check if a student is replying to another student's response, at the top of the page, click on the **CLASSMATE ANSWERS** tab:

3. Click on the **Reply** icon below the response:

4. Type the reply and click on the **POST** button:

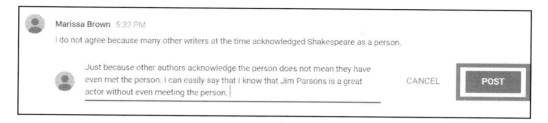

5. The reply is now visible under the post:

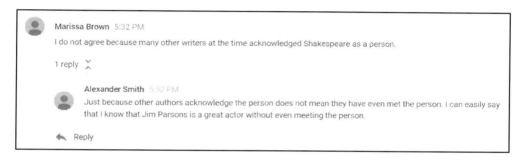

Collapsing replies

If the replies to responses become unruly, click on the reply count with converging arrows directly below the student's response to collapse all replies for that response:

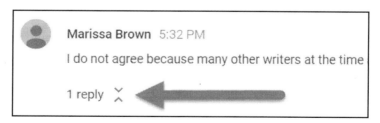

Creating multiple choice questions

Question posts can either be short answer or they can be multiple choice. To switch between short answer, which is the default option, and multiple choice, use the first drop-down menu in the question options, as shown here:

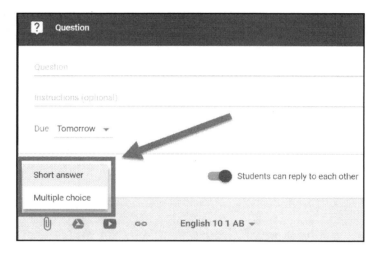

Each question can only have a single multiple choice question. The Chapter 7, *Google Forms for Multiple Choice and Fill-in-the-blank Assignments* shows how to create assignment posts with several multiple choice questions. After selecting the multiple choice option, radio buttons will appear below the question options. To add more multiple choice options, click on **Add option** in the list:

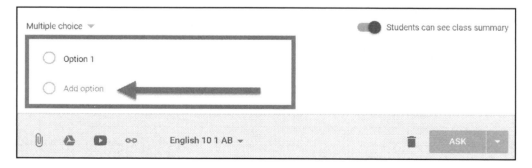

Multiple choice questions only have one option: **Students can see class summary**. The results will display on the post after the student has submitted their responses. An example of this option, which is enabled by default, is shown here:

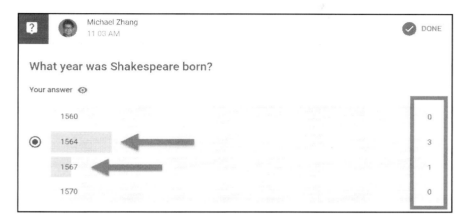

In the preceding screenshot, the darker grey sections on the left visually represent the number of times the choice is selected, while the numbers on the right indicate the total number of students who selected that option.

When immediate feedback is bad

During my teaching, I found that disabling immediate feedback provided more meaningful feedback than letting students see the class summary immediately. The students who completed the question quickly did not see the rest of the results without refreshing Google Classroom and the stragglers could wait and see what most of the class selected and choose accordingly. Instead, I found that revealing the summary after the majority of the students had completed the question worked better. Clicking on the title of a published multiple choice question post will go to the summary of responses. More about this page is in the next section.

Once all the necessary fields are filled and the appropriate question options are set, clicking on the **ASK** button will post the question.

Grading a question

The Question post allows teachers to track which students have responded to the question, as well as assign grades to those responses. Use the following steps to assign a grade:

1. Click on the title of the question:

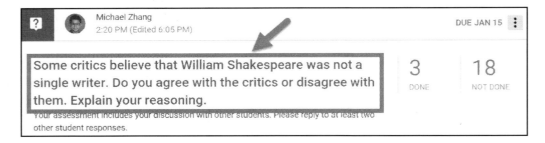

2. In the menu, click on the **100 points** drop-down menu to change how many points the question is worth:

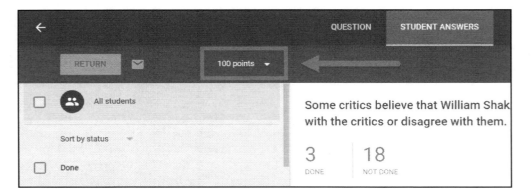

Grading the question will be easier if you decide how many points the question is worth before you begin grading. Google Classroom will notify already graded students when the total points of a question or assignment, changes and it does not give an option to adjust already graded questions to the new point total. Therefore, you will have to go back and change all the previously graded questions to the equivalent value for the new total:

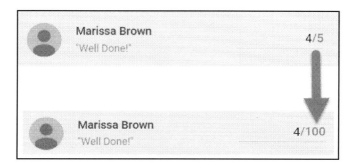

For the Question and Assignment post, the total points must be a numeric value. In Canada, many primary schools use a letter grade system to assess students. If your system is similar, a solution is to relate letter grades to a number value. For example, an A grade will be 4 points, a B grade, 3 points, and so on.

3. Assign the grade to the **Add Grade** line beside the student. Continue assigning a grade to students until all students are graded:

Google Classroom orders the students according to whether the question is completed. However, you can change the student list to order by the student's first or last names by using the drop down menu directly above the student list:

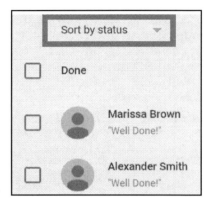

4. As grades are assigned to students, the checkbox beside the students will be checked. To return the graded question to the students, click on the **RETURN** button in the menu. Google Classroom will notify only students who have their checkboxes checked:

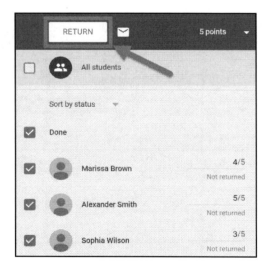

5. A dialog box will appear listing all the students whose graded questions will be returned. There is also a line to add a private comment. Each student will receive the private comment separately:

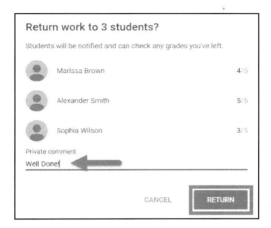

If you want to give individual feedback using the **Private comment** feature, you must return the assignments one at a time.

6. When you have completed grading all the student submissions, you can export the grades from Google Classroom into a spreadsheet. Click on the Settings gear above the student responses and select **Download these grades as a CSV**:

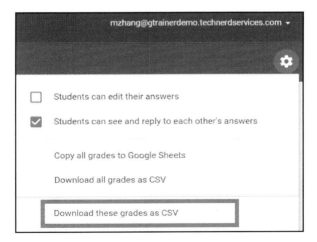

The two other options, **Copy all grades to Google Sheets** and **Download all grades as CSV,** will export all Question and Assignment grades within the class.

Leaving a question ungraded

The Question post also has an option to leave it ungraded. When returning the question, you will still be able to give feedback with the private comments:

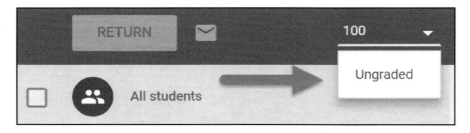

Viewing the returned grade

Once the question is returned to the students, they will be able to view the grade and private comments. Students can access the returned question by clicking on the provided link in the e-mail notification or by clicking on the title of the Question post in the Stream. Furthermore, the Question post in the Stream will also indicate in the heading that the question has been returned:

The student's Answer page will display the grade in a bubble on the right and the private comment below replies to the student response:

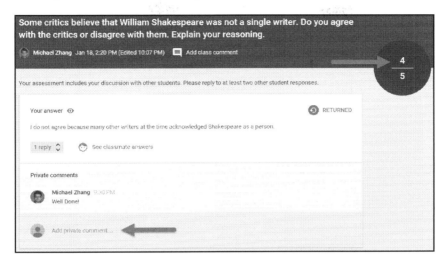

Students are able to add a follow up private comment after the question is returned. This private comment thread is similar to a student following up on a paper assignment in person.

Summary

The Question post provides several tools that enhance what you can do with the Stream to promote discussion within your class. It allows you to easily track which students have responded to the question that is posed and grade those responses. When integrating Question posts into your teaching, they can be used to enhance class discussions as well as promote out-of-class discussion for your students.

You are now able to create short answer and multiple choice Question posts within the Stream of your classes, assign a due date, and grade and return the questions with feedback. Students are now able to reply to each other's responses and your feedback. The grades, student responses, and feedback are all stored in the post, which can be easily found in the Stream.

In the next chapter, we will explore the final post type, the Assignment post. With this type of post, students will be able to respond by submitting documents.

5
Handing out and Taking in Assignments

In the previous chapters, you have learned how to use the Announcement and Question posts. In this chapter, you will learn the final post type: the Assignment post. This post allows you to assign documents stored in Google Drive, have students turn in the assignments, and then grade the assignments. This chapter will focus on how to assign and take in assignments because the grading process is similar to grading a Question post. However, there are some additional features available when grading assignments rather than questions, which the next chapter will explore. Furthermore, this question type heavily incorporates Google Docs and Google Drive, two additional apps in GAFE suite.

In this chapter, we will explore the following topics:

- Components of an Assignment post
- Sharing files in assignments
- Viewing files in Google Classroom and Google Drive
- How students turn in assignments
- How students add additional files to assignments

Creating an Assignment post

Similar to the Question post, many of the Assignment post's features are found in all three post types. If you are not reading the chapters in order, consider reading `Chapter 3`, *Sending Your First Announcement* and `Chapter 4`, *Starting a Discussion with Questions*.

To create an Assignment post, complete the following steps:

1. In the Stream, click on the **+** icon and then click on **Create assignment**:

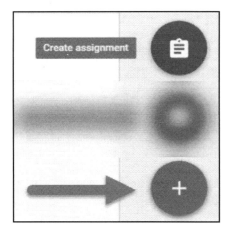

2. Fill in the **Title** and **Instructions** fields:

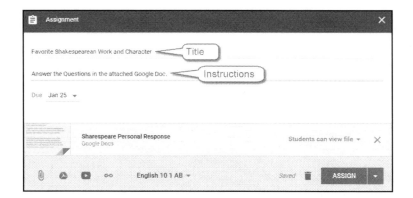

3. Use the **Due** menu to set up a due date and time:

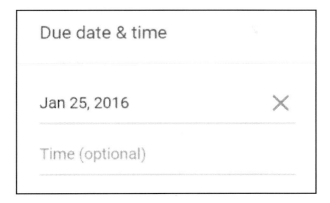

4. Use the **Upload a file to attach** or **Attach Google Drive** item icons to add files to the assignment. (This step is covered extensively in Chapter 3, *Sending Your First Announcement*.):

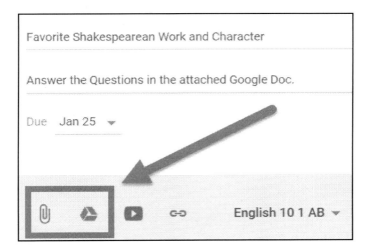

5. Use the class drop-down menu to select additional classes and then click on the **ASSIGN** button to post the assignment:

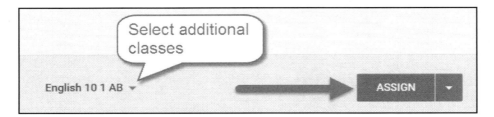

While not necessary, attaching files to an Assignment post separates its features from the Question post. Where the Question post allows grading of student responses to the post, the Assignment post allows grading of the files attached to it. In the following screenshot, you will see that the Assignment post, like the Question post, also tracks how many students have turned in the assignment:

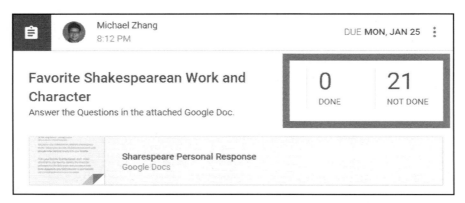

Sharing files in assignments

If you attach a file from your computer or Google Drive, you will notice an additional option beside the file that is not present in other post types. This new option, displayed in the following screenshot, allows you to choose how students receive this file:

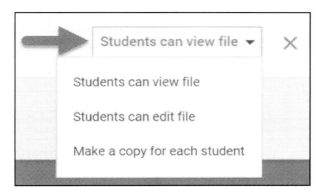

Each sharing option allows a different level of student interaction:

- **Student can view file**: This does not let students interact with this file. They are only able to read, download, or print the file.

  You can further prevent students from downloading or printing the file. However, those are advanced settings found in Google Drive and are beyond the scope of this book.

- **Students can edit file**: This allows all students to edit the same file. Therefore, you and your students will see each other's changes in real-time.
- **Make a copy for each student**: This will create a copy of the file in your Google Drive for each student. Students will not see what other students write in the document.

Choosing when to use which sharing permission depends on the purpose of the file. For example, if students are practicing editing a document, an assignment can be similar to the one in the following screenshot:

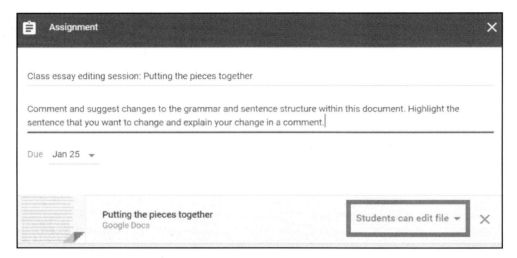

Another example is if you want students to critically respond to a work. You can attach some files as **Students can view file** and then attach the document that you want them to complete as **Make a copy for each student,** as shown here:

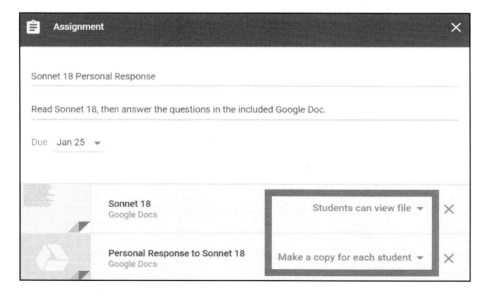

To utilize the full features of the Assignment post, ensure that the each file you assign with **Make a copy for each student** is a document created in Google Docs or converted into the Google Docs format. Students will only be able to edit the Google Docs file formats for Docs, Sheets, and Slides.

Viewing student files

The Assignment post has greater complexity than the other posts because there are files associated with the assignment. There are two different locations to access files turned in by students: Google Classroom and Google Drive.

Viewing student files in Google Classroom

To access student files in Google Classroom, regardless of whether they have turned in their work or not, follow these steps:

1. In the Stream, click on the title of the post:

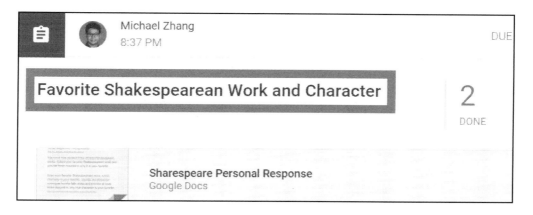

2. You will now be on the **STUDENT WORK** page. In the left-hand student list, click on the name of the student:

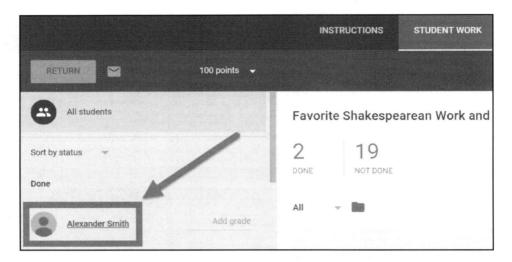

3. Click on the file you want to view:

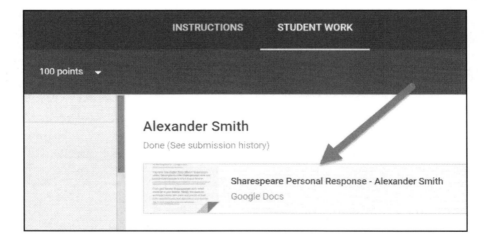

When you attach a file using the **Make a copy for each student** setting, the copies of the file will not be created until the student accesses the assignment. Therefore, you may have some students that do not have an assignment file created when you view the **STUDENT WORK** page, as shown in the following screenshot:

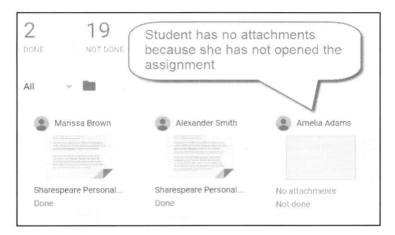

If the files are available, another method of viewing files from students is to click on them in the main section of the **STUDENT WORK** page, as shown in the following screenshot:

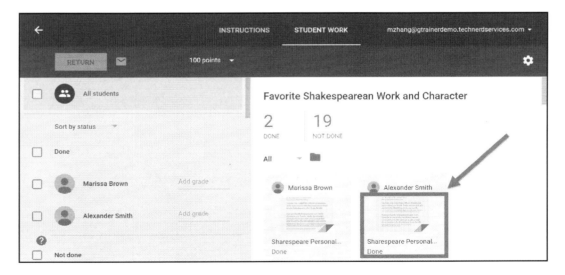

Viewing student files on the Google Classroom mobile app

The Google Classroom mobile app is another method to view student files. If you have a smartphone or tablet, viewing student files on your mobile device is a great way to multitask during class time. I have opened student files on my mobile device while managing the class countless times. Changes are visible in real time so that you can see the changes that the students are making without having to look over shoulders. The following steps will use the Google Classroom app on Apple's iOS. Using the app on Google's Android will use similar steps:

1. On the Home screen, Tap the **Classroom** app:

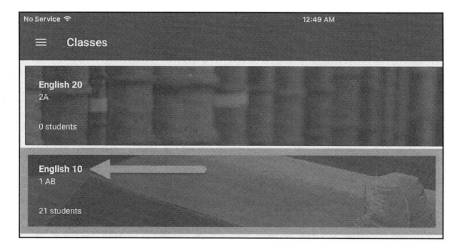

2. Tap on the class:

3. In the Stream, tap on the title of the assignment:

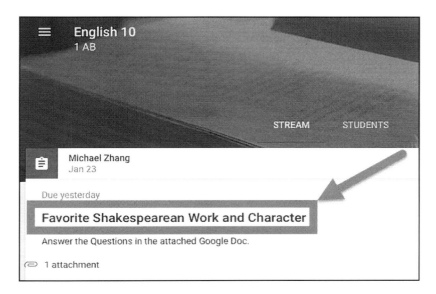

4. Tap on the **STUDENT WORK** tab:

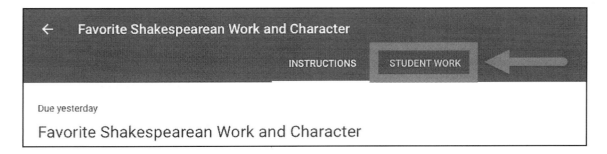

5. Tap on the student's name. Then tap on the assignment:

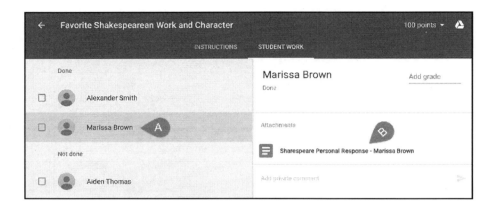

6. The file will open in Google Docs, as shown here:

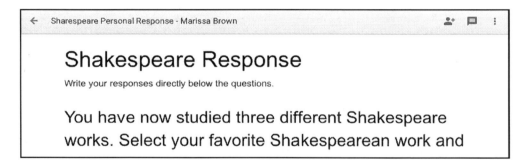

In Apple's iOS, the first time you open a file from Google Classroom, dialog boxes will appear after step 5 asking permission to access the Google Drive and Google Docs apps on the iPad or iPhone.

On Apple's iOS and Google's Android, the Google Drive and Google Docs apps must be present on the device. If they are not already installed, refer to Chapter 2, *Inviting Students to Their Virtual Classroom*, for comprehensive instructions.

Viewing student files in Google Drive

Google Drive is an online file storage and management app for Google Apps. All files uploaded or created in Google Classroom are stored in Google Drive. Since it is possible to view student files directly from the Google Drive app, it can be more convenient to access student files there if you already use Google Drive frequently.

There is no limit to how much data you can store in Google Drive for GAFE and **Google Apps for Work** (**GAFW**) accounts; however, standard Google accounts (e-mails that end in *@gmail.com*) have a 15 GB total storage limit. For standard Google accounts, Google Docs, Sheets, and Slides files do not contribute to the 15 GB maximum.

Use the following steps to view student files from the Google Drive app:

1. In Google Chrome, navigate to `drive.google.com`. An alternative is to click on the App Launcher in another Google app (such as Gmail or Google Calendar) and then click on the **Drive** icon:

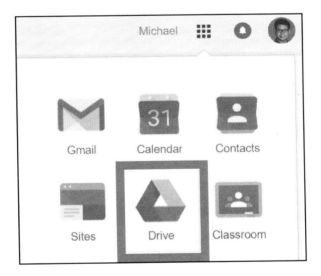

2. Click on the folder named **Classroom:**

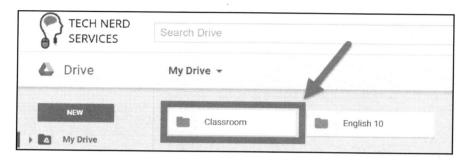

3. Click on the folder with the class name:

4. Click on the folder with the same title as the Assignment post:

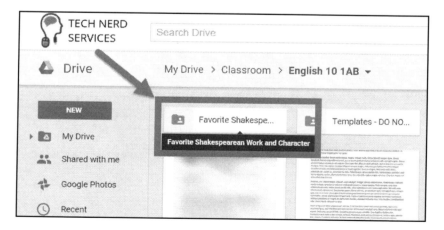

5. Click on the assignment you wish to view.

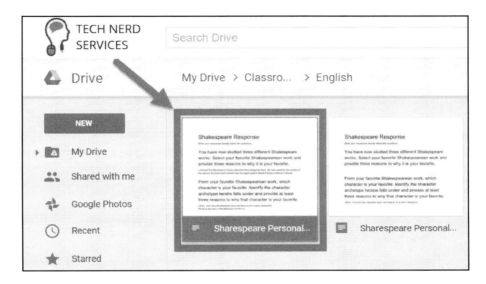

6. The file will open in a new tab in Google Docs:

Viewing files in a details list

Google Drive defaults to a thumbnail view of the files. In the preceding screenshot, you can see that the filename is cut off, obscuring the student name. Click on the List View icon shown here in the menu:

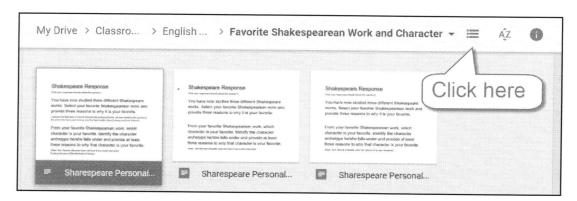

Your files will no longer show a thumbnail of the first page. Instead, only the file format icon and the filename will be visible. Additionally, two columns containing more details about the document will appear. The following screenshot shows the List View of Google Drive:

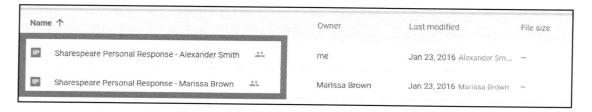

Turning in assignments

If students are new to using Google Classroom, they may also need guidance for turning in their assignments through Google Classroom. During my time teaching, I learned that if I did not explicitly show students how to turn in assignments, I would receive them incomplete or through e-mail. To save extra work in collecting assignments, take a few moments at the beginning of the first few assignments to show students how to properly turn in assignments. After assigning the assignment, have a student log into a computer connected to a projector so that you can show the students the steps to correctly submit the assignment.

For assignments with Google Docs, sharing files with the **Make a copy for each student** setting is the simplest method for students to turn in an assignment. As with the preceding example, Favorite Shakespearean Work and Character, the assignment contains one Google Doc that the student needs to edit. Since it was shared with **Make a copy for each student**, when the student opens the Google Doc, a **Turn in** button will appear in the menu, as shown here:

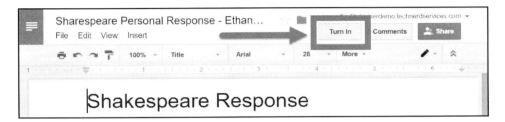

When the student finishes the assignment, they can click on the **TURN IN** button in the Google Doc document and they can confirm the submission in the dialog box that appears, as shown here:

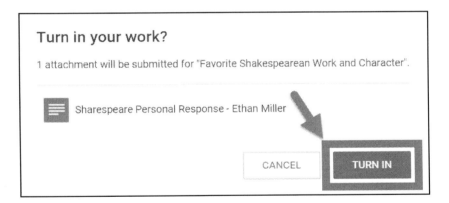

The first few assignments created through Google Docs always use this method exclusively. This method is the easiest method for students to turn in assignments because there are fewer steps for the student. Once students are comfortable turning in Google Doc assignments with the **Make a copy for each student** setting, then I will provide more complex assignments where students can add additional files to the assignment.

Adding additional files to assignments

As students become more proficient in turning in assignments in Google Classroom, they will be able to complete more complex assignments. Students are able to add additional files from Google Drive to their assignments before turning them in. To do that, guide them through the following steps:

1. In Google Classroom, click on the title of the assignment:

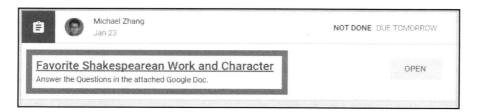

2. Click on the **Add** drop-down menu. Then, click on the **Google Drive** icon or text:

3. Navigate to the file and click on the **Add** button:

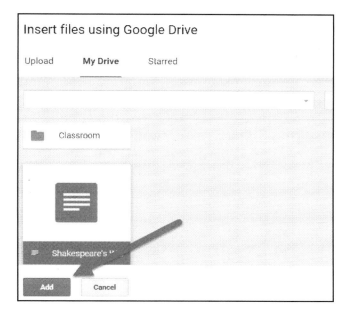

There are additional steps if a student wants to upload a file from their computer. In the **Add** drop-down menu, the student will need to click on the **File** icon instead of the Google Drive icon, as shown here:

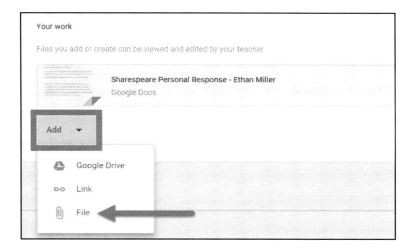

Once they find the file, they will need to click on the **Upload** button in the Google Drive dialog box to upload and add the files to the assignment:

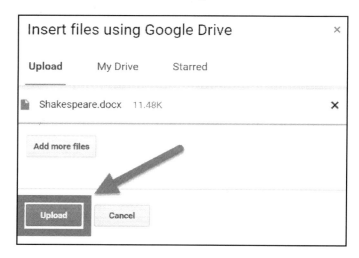

Using mobile devices with assignments

If students use the Google Classroom app, they will be able to use additional features found within the Google Classroom mobile app. On the mobile app, students can tap the **+Add attachment** link in the assignment, as shown here:

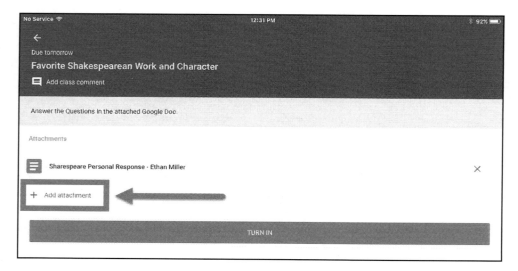

The menu that appears will have an option to use the camera:

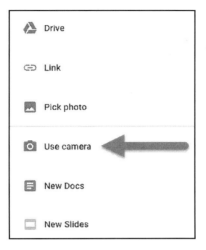

Using this camera feature, students can take pictures or video and attach them to the assignment:

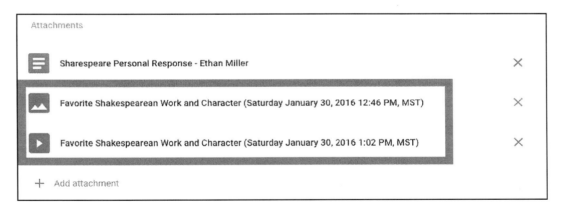

Using mobile devices with Google Classroom fosters creative learning and assessment. If there are enough mobile devices in your class, students can submit skits, songs, oral analyses, laboratory demonstrations, graphs, and more, by simply taking pictures or recording video directly from their smartphone or tablet. If there are not enough mobile devices, consider incorporating these assignments in group work.

Unsubmitting and resubmitting assignments

At any time after they have submitted their assignment, students can make changes to their assignment. First, the student needs to unsubmit the assignment, which they can do by clicking on the title of the Assignment post in the Stream. Below their work there is an **UNSUBMIT** button, as shown here:

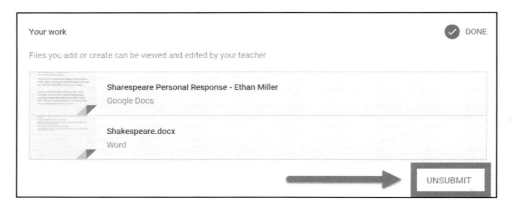

Once the assignment is unsubmitted, students will be able to make changes to their files before turning them in again. If students unsubmit and turn in their assignment after the due date, Google Classroom still flags the assignment as late. At the time of writing, there is no way to disable the unsubmit button.

Once a student has unsubmitted an assignment, you will be able to see when students turn in new submissions. In the Student Work tab of the assignment, clicking on **See submission history**, shown here, will display a list of when the student turned in the assignment:

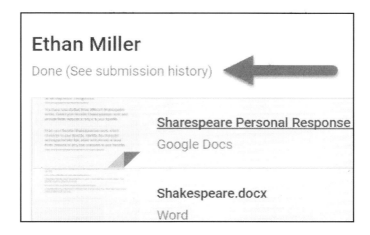

Turning in assignments late

Students are able to turn in assignments late. However, if they do, Google Classroom will flag the assignment as late. At the time of writing, there is no simple method for creating a hard deadline where students are unable to submit assignments after the deadline. The following screenshot shows an example of how Google Classroom indicates a late assignment submission:

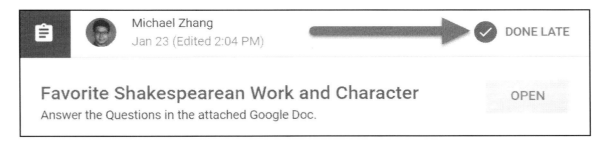

File ownership for assignments

Just like with physical assignments, ownership of the student's assignment transfers to the teacher when students turn in assignments. Therefore, if you view a student's file in Google Drive, turned in assignments will display **me** for the owner instead of the student's name:

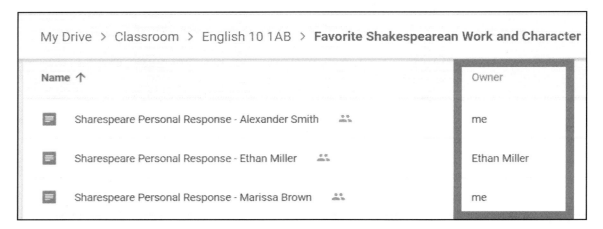

While seemingly inconsequential, students have limited privileges with turned in files. For example, they will not see any changes or comments to the assignment until it is returned to them.

If students unsubmit their assignment after you have graded it but before you have returned it, the student will be able to see your changes or comments, but will not see the grade. Grades are only visible to the students when the assignment is returned.

Another limitation for students is that they are only able to view the turned in files and cannot make any changes unless they unsubmit the assignment. Thus, having ownership transfer to you until you grade and return the assignment ensures that there are no unexpected surprises during the grading process.

Summary

Assignment posts allow you to manage and consolidate your assignments in a single location. You neither have to keep track of which students have turned in their assignments and which ones have not, nor do you need to worry about misplacing assignments at home, in the classroom, or somewhere in between. In addition, you are no longer limited to print text. Now you are able to attach any type of file, such as images and videos, links to websites, or YouTube videos.

You are now able to create Assignment posts and know the ins and outs of adding content to the posts, how students turn in assignments, and where you can find all the assignments in Google Classroom and Google Drive. You have learned how to recognize when students unsubmit their assignments or turn them in late.

In the next two chapters, we will go through various methods of grading assignments in Google Classroom. We will focus on providing meaningful feedback and tools to speed up the grading process.

6
Grading Written Assignments in a Flash

Now that you have your student files, it's time to grade them. Marking assignments is one of the necessary evils for teachers. There is never time during the day to mark all the assignments students turn in. Therefore, we teachers also have constant homework, where we are marking assignments at home. Thankfully, Google Classroom and other Google Apps help reduce the time it takes to grade and return assignments. (Not to mention, reducing your environmental impact by reducing paper use within your classroom.) This chapter will focus on grading written assignments, whereas the next chapter will focus on creating and grading multiple choice, numeric response, and fill-in-the-blank type questions. Since written assignments are turned in from Google Docs, providing feedback will use features found within the Google Docs app to enhance the grading process. These features include comments, suggesting mode, and revision history. Furthermore, third-party apps developed by *New Visions for Public Schools* provide even more time-saving features when grading written assignments that use rubrics. You will learn how to install Doctopus and Goobric, create Goobric-compatible templates, ingest assignments with Doctopus, and grade them with Goobric. Once you are familiar with these tools, you will spend less time grading than ever before.

Assigning a grade

The Google Classroom page for assignment submissions is the same as the page for the Question post submissions you learned about in `Chapter 4`, *Starting an Online Discussion with Questions*. Check out that chapter for in-depth steps regarding changing how many points an assignment is worth and other tips. To assign and return an assignment, follow these steps:

1. Click on the title of the Assignment post you wish to grade:

2. In the main section of the assignments page, click on the student's assignment to view the document. (If there are multiple attachments, you will be taken to a list of the attachments.):

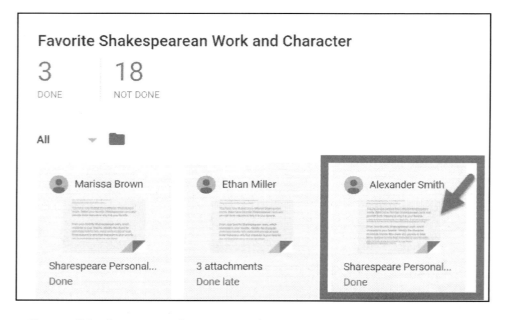

Compatible documents that open within Google Docs or media files will play in a new tab of Google Chrome. All other files will be downloaded to your computer. When you finish evaluating the document, close its tab in Google Chrome to return to Google Classroom.

3. Assign a grade to the student in the student list on the left sidebar:

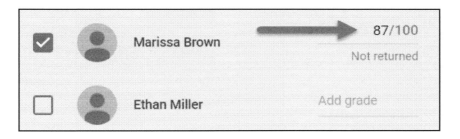

4. When you are ready to return the assignments, check the checkbox beside the students whose assignments you want to return. Then click on the **RETURN** button at the top of the student list:

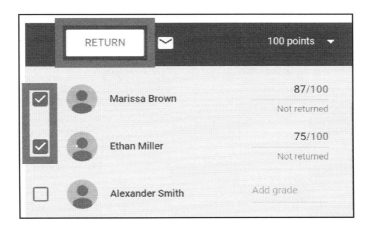

To select all students within the class, click on the checkbox beside all students in the student list. Also, if the student list is sorted by status, you can select all students who are done or not done by checking the checkbox beside the appropriate header.

Once the assignment is returned, as in the Questions post, students will receive an e-mail notification as well as be able to see the feedback in Google Classroom.

Providing feedback with private messages and comments

Usually, teachers are encouraged to provide meaningful feedback in addition to a grade so that students can receive guidance to improve their work. You can provide written feedback through private messages within the Assignment post, and comments within the submitted Google Docs document.

Private messages are the feedback for the entire assignment. They are similar to writing a couple of sentences at the end of an essay or a lab report. To add a private message, follow these instructions:

1. On the assignment page, click on the student's name in the Student list:

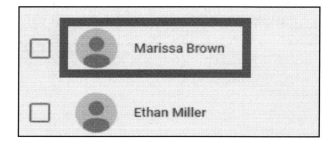

2. Below the list of attachments, click on the **Add private comment...** section:

3. Add your private message and then click on the **POST** button:

Adding comments to student files

While you can add private comments to the assignment, follow these steps to add comments to the content of a Google Docs document. This method of feedback allows you to highlight specific parts of the assignment to comment upon. Use these steps to add a comment to a Google Doc document:

1. On the assignment page, click on the assignment below the student's name in the assignment list. The Google Docs document will open in a new tab:

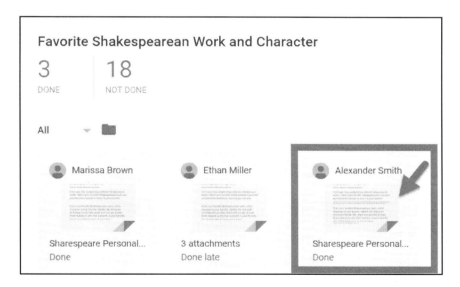

If there are multiple attachments to the assignment, you will need to click on the file from a list of all attachments.

2. Highlight the text you want to comment and click on the **Add a comment** icon that appears on the right of the Google Docs document:

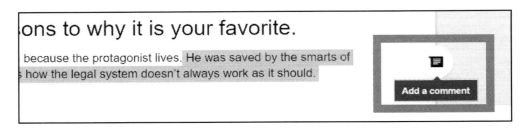

If an **Add a comment** icon does not appear on the side of the document, use the **Add a comment** icon in the toolbar:

3. Type in your comment and click on the **Save** button when complete:

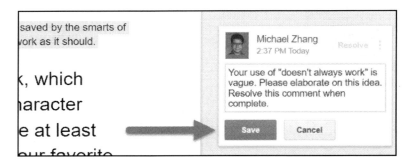

Comments have a **Resolve** button, shown as follows, which anyone who can edit the document can click:

After the assignments are returned to the students, they can make necessary changes and resolve the comment. It is important to instruct students in class or in the comment to resolve the comment when they have addressed it. When comments are resolved, you will receive an e-mail to notify you that the assignment is ready for reassessment.

Using comments to collaborate

The comments feature is a useful tool for students to edit each other's work. Students can share their work with each other and evaluate one another's work. Editors can reply to each other's comments within the document. You and students can have side conversations within threads of comments to promote collaborative learning.

Suggesting changes to a student file

Another method of adding comments is to suggest changes to the text. Google Docs will record changes you make to the document. This method of feedback is great for providing feedback for sentence structure, wordiness and conciseness in essays, lab reports, and other long documents. The **Suggesting** feature is similar to **Track Changes** in Microsoft Word. To enable suggesting mode in a Google Docs document, click on the editing menu and select **Suggesting,** as shown in the following screenshot:

Now when you write in the document, it will display the changes and add a comment:

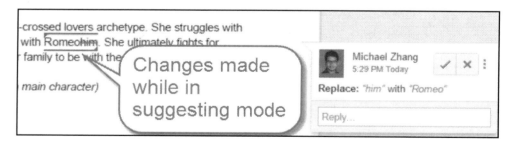

Saving your comments

When grading several papers, you may write the same or similar comments for several students. Therefore, use another Google Docs document to save your comments so that you can copy and paste comments. Some keyboards also include macros buttons, which can store comments.

Monitoring student progress with revision history

Revision history takes snapshots of a Google Docs document as content is added. It is a digital paper trail that allows you and the students to view previous versions of the document. While it saddens me, students do occasionally cheat on assignments. If you are suspicious of the authenticity of a written assignment that a student submits, checking the revision history of a document may provide clues to whether the student copied and pasted a premade assignment into the document. To activate **Revision history**, click on the **See revision history** option in the **File** menu, as shown here:

If the student wrote the assignment in Google Docs, there will be a number of revisions in the right sidebar and you will see highlighting of text that the student has added within the revision. Following is an example of the revision history of a Google Docs document that a student completed:

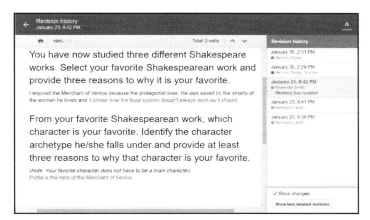

If a student copies an assignment, there will only be two revisions available—a blank document and the complete document.

For smaller assignments, click on the **Show more detailed revisions** button at the bottom of the right sidebar. It will reveal more revision increments.

Using a rubric to grade assignments

When grading long documents such as essays and lab reports, you may use a rubric to provide feedback to your students. However, Google Classroom does not have features that allow you to assign grades in this manner. Third-parties such as *New Visions for Public Schools* have developed add-ons and extensions that allow you to grade assignments in Google Classroom. In order to mark efficiently with rubrics in Google Docs, you will need to set up the Chrome extension Goobric and the Google Sheets add-on Doctopus. While there are several steps in the initial setup for Goobric and Doctopus, once they are installed, the grading process goes smoothly. A Spanish teacher at my school used Goobric and Doctopus to grade over 700 student assignments within a semester. She claimed that this system saved her over 100 hours of marking than previous semesters. Goobric allows you to see your rubric and the student assignment within a single screen. Furthermore, when you have completed grading, Goobric will insert the rubric within the Google Docs assignment. In this section, you will complete the following:

- Installing Goobric and Doctopus
- Creating a Rubric
- Ingesting a Classroom assignment
- Grading the assignments using Goobric

Installing Doctopus and Goobric

While there is no preferred order to install Doctopus and Goobric, one important step is to first sign into Google Chrome. Because Goobric is a Google Chrome extension, it will use the account that is signed into Google Chrome, which is not necessarily the account that is visible in a tab. Follow the following steps to sign into Google Chrome:

1. Click on the user icon:

2. Click on the **Sign in to Chrome** button:

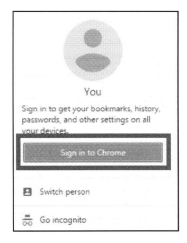

3. Enter your e-mail, password, and click on the **Sign in** button:

4. If a pop-up appears with the **Link your Chrome data to this account?** heading, click on the **Link Data** button:

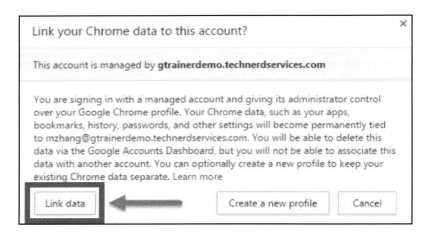

5. A pop-up will appear indicating that you are signed into Google Chrome and your name will appear where the user icon was in the Google Chrome window heading. Click on the **OK, got it** button to close the pop-up:

Signing into Chrome has additional benefits. Your account will save your bookmarks, settings, apps, and extensions so that if you log into Google Chrome on another computer, your account will sync so that you do not have to redo your saved settings.

Now that Google Chrome is linked to your account, you can use the following steps to install Goobric from the Chrome Web Store:

1. In a new tab, click on the **Apps** icon in the bookmarks menu:

2. Click on the **Web Store** icon in the center of the screen:

   If you cannot find the **Apps** icon in the bookmarks menu, simply type `https://ch rome.google.com/webstore` in the address bar.

3. In the search bar in the left sidebar, type `Goobric` and hit the *Enter* key:

4. Under the **Extensions** section of the search results, click on the **+ ADD TO CHROME** button in the **Goobric Web App Launcher** extension:

5. A pop-up will appear. Click on the **Add extension** button:

6. When installed, you will see the Goobric icon beside the address bar:

Goobric is now successfully installed in Chrome and an account profile is associated with it. If the following text appears, double-check that the user profile is logged into Google Chrome as well as the Google web apps:

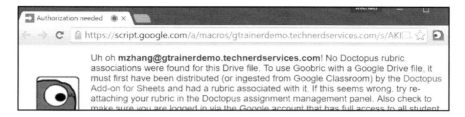

The final step is to install the add-on Doctopus, which will take an assignment in Google Classroom and import it into a Google Sheet. Use the following steps to install Doctopus:

1. In a new tab, click on the App Launcher and click on the **Sheets** icon:

If there is no icon for **Sheets**, type `https://sheets.google.com` in the address bar.

2. Click on a **Blank** template:

3. In the menu, click on the**Add-ons** menu and then click on **Get add-ons…**:

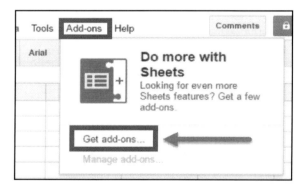

4. In the search field, type **Doctopus** and hit the *Enter* key:

5. In the Doctopus add-on, click the **+ FREE** button:

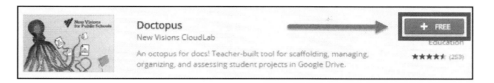

6. A pop-up will appear asking you to allow the permissions this add-on requires to function. Scroll to the bottom of the list and click on the **Allow** button:

7. On the Google Sheet, a pop-up will appear confirming the successful installation of Doctopus:

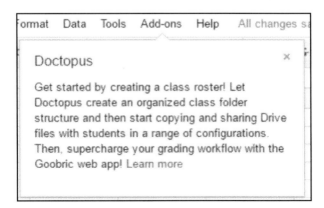

8. If the Doctopus sidebar appears, click on **x** to close the sidebar. (We will reopen it in a new sheet after creating rubrics.):

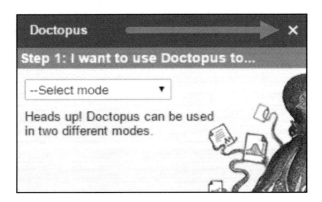

You have successfully signed into Google Chrome and installed the Goobric extension and Doctopus add-on. Once these steps are complete, you do not need to repeat them in the future.

Creating a rubric

Goobric uses both numeric and non-numeric rubrics. The *New Visions for Public Schools* Doctopus website (`http://cloudlab.newvisions.org/add-ons/doctopus`) has a link to Goobric's frequently asked questions (FAQs) page. These FAQs include more information about the rubric formatting, as well as troubleshooting tips if you encounter any problems.

 The Doctopus website has YouTube videos that demonstrate several of its features.

Rubrics must be created in Google Sheets before you can start marking. To create a numeric rubric, use the following instructions:

1. If you have been following along, you should still be in a Google Sheet. Otherwise, use the previous section's steps to open a Google Sheet.

2. At the top of the Google Sheet, click on **Untitled spreadsheet** and name the spreadsheet:

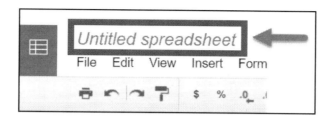

3. The first column displays the categories, whereas the first row displays the grade value. *Cell A1 must not have any information.* Starting with *A2*, fill each cell with the criteria of your rubric. If these cells are filled with anything other than numbers, the rubric will be treated as a non-numeric rubric:

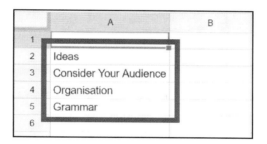

4. Starting at B1, fill each cell of the first row with the number value of each criteria:

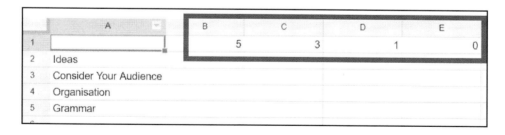

5. Fill the remaining cells of the rubric with the necessary assessment descriptors:

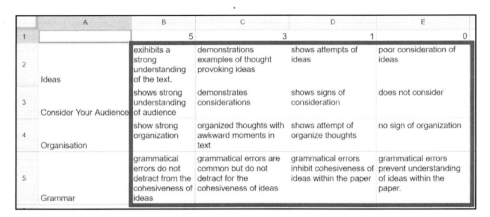

	A	B	C	D	E
1		5	3	1	0
2	Ideas	exihibits a strong understanding of the text.	demonstrations examples of thought provoking ideas	shows attempts of ideas	poor consideration of ideas
3	Consider Your Audience	shows strong understanding of audience	demonstrates considerations	shows signs of consideration	does not consider
4	Organisation	show strong organization	organized thoughts with awkward moments in text	shows attempt of organize thoughts	no sign of organization
5	Grammar	grammatical errors do not detract from the cohesiveness of ideas	grammatical errors are common but do not detract for the cohesiveness of ideas	grammatical errors inhibit cohesiveness of ideas within the paper	grammatical errors prevent understanding of ideas within the paper.

Goobric also allows you to grade with non-numeric rubrics. In the first row, use grading codes instead of number values:

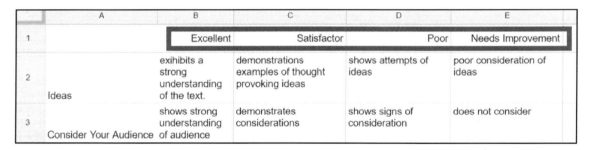

	A	B	C	D	E
1		Excellent	Satisfactor	Poor	Needs Improvement
2	Ideas	exihibits a strong understanding of the text.	demonstrations examples of thought provoking ideas	shows attempts of ideas	poor consideration of ideas
3	Consider Your Audience	shows strong understanding of audience	demonstrates considerations	shows signs of consideration	does not consider

Similar to setting up Doctopus and Goobric, once your rubrics are converted into Goobric-compatible rubrics, you will not need to redo them for each assignment. You can reuse rubrics on any number of assignments.

Ingesting and grading assignments with Goobric

Now that all the preparation is complete, you are ready to begin grading an assignment with Goobric. Follow these steps to begin grading your assignment:

1. Open a new Google Sheet. If you are still in the rubric Google Sheet, click on the **File** menu, then in the **New** submenu, click on **Spreadsheet**.

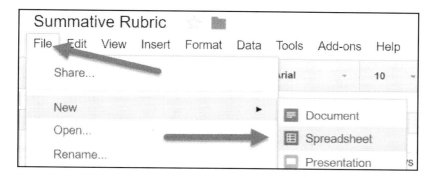

While it is possible to use the same Google Sheet as the rubric you just created, keeping it as a separate file will make it easier to find it in the future if you choose to use the same rubric on different assignments.

2. At the top of the Google Sheet, click on **Untitled spreadsheet** and name the spreadsheet:

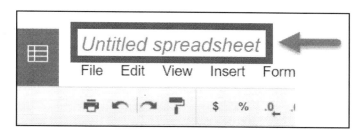

3. In the **Add-ons** menu, click on **Launch** in the **Doctopus** submenu:

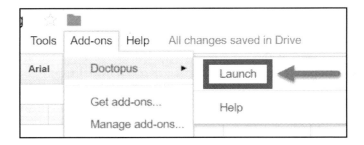

4. In the drop-down menu, select **ingest a Google Classroom assignment**. The bottom half of the Doctopus sidebar will change:

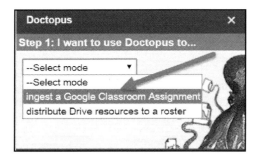

5. In the bottom half of the Doctopus sidebar, select the appropriate class in the class drop-down menu, then select the appropriate assignment. Finally, click on the **Ingest assignment** button:

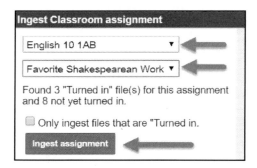

Before the **Ingest assignment** button, there is a checkbox to allow you to select whether Doctopus will ingest all assignments or only those that are turned in.

As shown in the following screenshot, Doctopus will create a new sheet with headers and student and assignment information. You do not need to make any changes to this information:

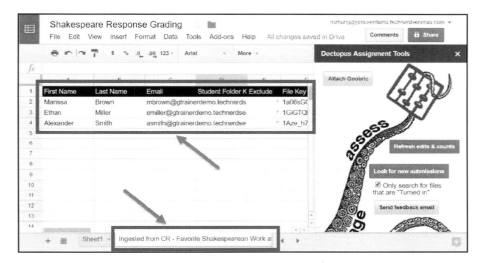

6. In the Doctopus sidebar, click on the **Attach Goobric** button:

7. You may see a pop-up with the heading **Goobric needs a moment of your attention**. At the time of writing, *New Visions for Public Schools* has released a new app, *Goobric for Students*, which allows students to assess each other's assignments. Click on the **Re-initialize Goobric** button:

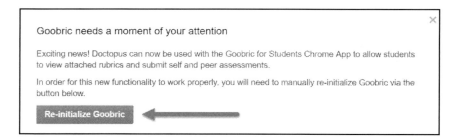

8. A pop-up will appear asking you to allow the permissions this add-on requires to function. Scroll to the bottom of the list and click on the **Allow** button:

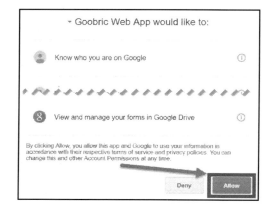

9. A confirmation message will appear in the tab. Close the tab:

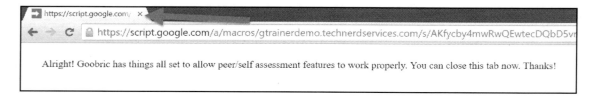

Steps 7 to 9 are only required once. Occasionally, Goobric and Doctopus will update and you may need to reauthorize the update similarly by performing these or similar steps. After the update, you may need to click on the **Attach Goobric** button a second time.

10. A pop-up will appear with the heading **Attach Goobric**. Click on the gray box with the Google Sheets icon to view sheets in your Google Drive. The next time you attach a Goobric to a Sheet, it will first display your recent Goobric rubrics:

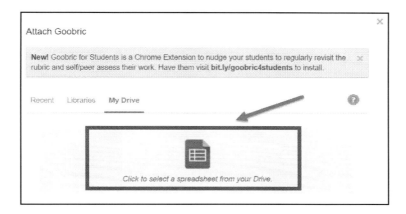

11. Select your rubric and then click on the **Select** button:

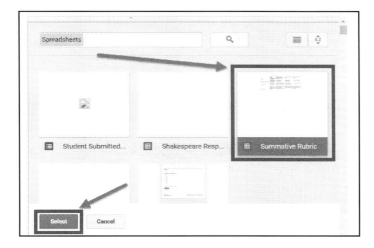

If you are having difficulty finding your rubric, use the search bar at the top of the pop-up.

12. The next screen of the pop-up will display the criteria of the rubric as well as provide checkboxes for additional settings, such as making the rubric viewable to students, allowing self or peer assessment, and sending an e-mail notification to students. Check or uncheck your desired settings and then click on the **Attach Rubric** button:

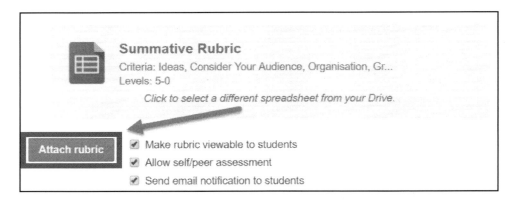

If you choose to send an e-mail notification to your students, they will receive an e-mail immediately with the link to the rubric as well as instructions to install the *Goobric for Students* Chrome extension for self/peer assessment, if those options are also selected.

13. The columns in the spreadsheet will change slightly. In the first student row, hover your mouse over the **Assess document** text of the **Goobric Link** heading. A link will appear above the cell. Click on the link to open the Google Docs document in Goobric:

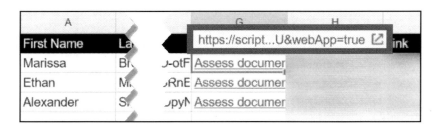

14. If it is the first time assessing an assignment with Goobric, a new pop-up will appear in Google Chrome requesting access to the computer's microphone. This step is optional and adds the feature of saving voice recordings as part of your evaluation. This feature is a great alternative to writing all your feedback. Click on **Allow** if you want to use this feature:

Re-enabling the microphone

If the microphone is already disabled in Goobric, click on the camera icon on the right-hand side of the omnibar and select the **Always allow** radio button, as shown in the following screenshot:

After clicking on the **Done** button, the page will need to be refreshed before the microphone activates.

Goobric grading features

Once you have clicked on the link from the Goobric link column, a new tab will appear with three distinct sections—the Goobric rubric, assignment comments, and the Google Docs document, as shown in the following screenshot:

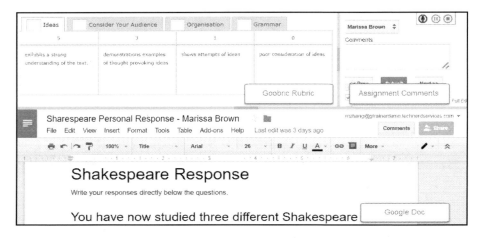

In the Google Docs document of the assignment, you are able to provide feedback through the methods discussed at the beginning of this chapter—adding comments and suggesting changes. The main advantage of Goobric is having the marking rubric visible on the same window. The rubric's criteria are the tabs in the rubric section, and you can switch between them. In order to select the point value, click on the necessary descriptor. As shown in the following screenshot, the rubric section will turn yellow to indicate that there are unsaved changes. This section will remain yellow until you submit your grades in Goobric:

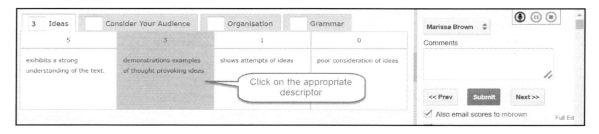

If you are using a numeric rubric, the point value for the corresponding criteria descriptor will appear in the tab. You are able to manually change this number if necessary. Goobric will highlight the two descriptors closest to the manually changed number. For example, the following screenshot shows the sample rubric with a **4** manually entered into the criteria value. Goobric will then highlight the **5** and **3** point descriptors:

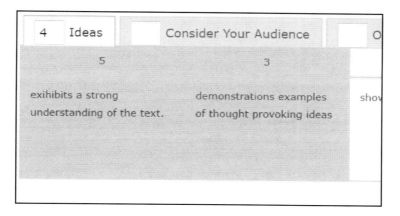

Once you have filled in the grading rubric, you can add assignment comments. These comments will appear at the bottom of the rubric, within the assignment. They are very similar to private comments in Google Classroom. One main difference is that you can record comments for your students to listen to instead of writing the comments. If you have been following along with all the steps in this chapter, Goobric will have access to your computer's microphone (if your computer has one). Click on the microphone button at the top of this section to record your audio feedback:

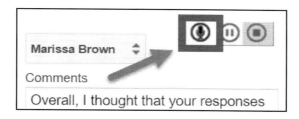

Once you are done recording, Goobric will save the file as an MP3 file and share it with the student. A link to the audio file will be visible in the assignment comments section, as shown in the following screenshot:

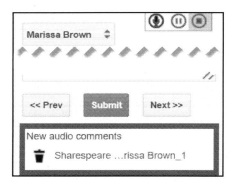

Now that you have added, typed, or recorded comments to the assignment, you are ready to submit the assignment. Submitting the assignment will add the rubric to the bottom of the Google Docs assignment, as well as the assignment comments and link to the audio feedback. Before you click on the **Submit** button, there are a few checkbox options. You can have Goobric notify the student with an e-mail that the assignment is graded, you can have the file permissions changed so that the student can comment on the assignment, and you can choose to auto-advance to the next assignment in the Google Sheet list when you click on the **Submit** button. The following screenshot displays the options in the assignment comments section:

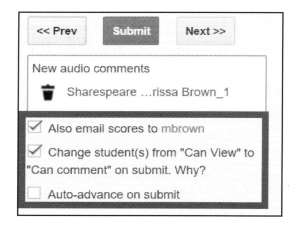

The default options for Goobric are displayed in the preceding screenshot. In my experience, I usually disable the emailing of the scores to the student and I enable the **Auto-advance on submit** option. I disable the e-mail scores to student option so that I can use the Google Classroom Return feature in the assignment to notify all the students when I complete marking all student work. (I sometimes change grading schemes partway through marking a class. Therefore, not notifying students early grants more flexibility in grading.) Furthermore, Google Classroom will automatically change the Google Docs ownership back to the student once the assignment is returned. Finally, **Auto-advance on submit** is a great time-saving feature. Following are the settings that I usually use in this section of Goobric:

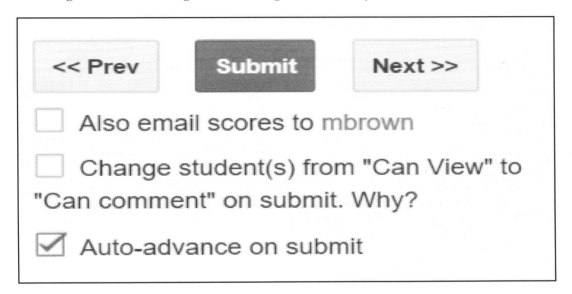

With these settings, once you click on the **Submit** button, the tab will load the next assignment on the list. Often, when I grade with Goobric, I am unaware of how many assignments I have already graded or how long each assignment takes. However, the amount of time I spend grading assignments using Goobric is definitely shorter than without it.

Once assignments are graded, the Google Sheet with Doctopus will create a new sheet with the assigned points, as shown in the following screenshot. The Goobric FAQs states that the scores sheet does not add all the points together in case teachers weigh criteria differently. Nevertheless, it is an easy method of viewing your progress with regard to how many assignments are graded:

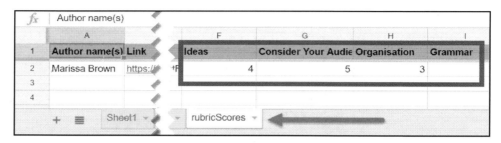

When you or your student's view their assignments, the rubric, assignment comments, and link to the audio file will be visible at the end of the assignment. The following screenshot is an example of what Goobric adds to the end of the assignment:

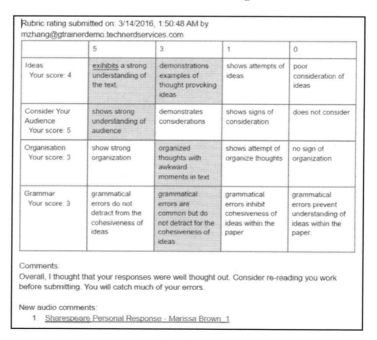

Customizing the layout of Goobric

Goobric includes tools to change its layout depending on your computer setup and preferences. One example is the ability to resize the frames in Goobric by clicking and dragging the center gray portion of any of the frames:

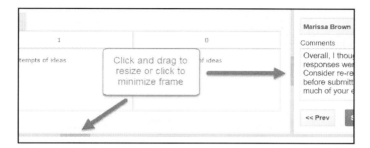

Furthermore, if you click on the gray section of the frames, the frames will minimize, which is great if you are using a smaller screen. Another customization available is changing the rubric section to display the entire rubric instead of the criteria by tabs, as shown here:

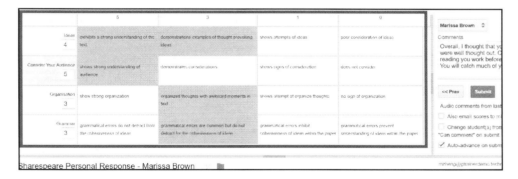

This layout may be more preferable when using a larger, or a high-pixel monitor. To switch the rubric view, hover your mouse at the top-right corner of the rubric section. A double-headed arrow button will appear; click on it to switch views:

Summary

In this chapter, you learned about the grading and assignment feedback features within Google Classroom. Then you enhanced those features with the commenting and suggesting features found within Google Docs. Next, you learned about Google Docs revision history, to view previous snapshots of a Google Docs document.

The latter half of the chapter focused on a set of third-party apps from *New Visions for Public Schools* that pulled assignments from Google Classroom and allowed them to be graded with a rubric. You learned how to install Doctopus and Goobric and create a Goobric-compatible rubric. Finally, you explored the features of Goobric such as audio feedback and auto-advancing.

Goobric is not without its quirks. Because it uses scripting, formulas created with Google Doc's formula editor often appear offset. Furthermore, if there are multiple Google Docs documents attached to an assignment, Doctopus will include each file into the Google Sheet, which can be cumbersome if students are attaching extra files or if they are not using a file of which you have made a copy for each student. However, its time-saving features outweigh these quirks. Thus, Google Classroom, Google Docs, Doctopus, and Goobric culminate into a system that streamlines how you mark long-format written assignments.

In the next chapter, we will explore how to use Google Forms to create multiple choice, numeric, and fill-in-the-blanks questions and another third party app, Flubaroo, to grade those forms.

7

Google Forms for Multiple Choice and Fill-in-the-blank Assignments

Now that we have explored how to grade written assignments using Doctopus and Goobric, the third-party app, Flubaroo will help grade multiple choice, fill-in-the-blank, and numeric questions. Before you can use Flubaroo, you will need to create the assignment and deploy it on Google Classroom. The Forms app of Google within the GAFE suite allows you to create online surveys, which you can use as assignments. Google Forms then outputs the values of the form into a Google Sheet, where the Google Sheet add-on, Flubaroo, then grades the assignment.

After using Google Forms and Flubaroo for assignments, you may decide to also use it for exams. However, while Google Forms provides a means for creating the assessment and Google Classroom allows you to easily distribute it to your students, *there is no method to maintain the security of the assessment*. Therefore, if you choose to use this tool for summative assessment, you will need to determine an appropriate level of security. (Often, there is nothing that prevents students from opening a new tab and searching for an answer or from messaging classmates.) For example, in my classroom, I adjusted the desks so that there was room at the back of the classroom to pace during a summative assessment. Additionally, some school labs include a teacher's desktop that includes software to monitor student desktops. Whatever method you choose, take precautions to ensure the authenticity of student results when assessing students online.

Google Forms is a vast Google app that requires its own book to fully explore its functionality. Therefore, the various features you will explore in this chapter will focus on the scope of creating and assessing multiple choice and fill-in-the-blank assignments. However, once you are familiar with Google Forms, you will find additional applications.

For example, in my school, I work with the administration to create forms to collect survey data from stakeholders such as staff, students, and parents. Recently, for our school's annual Open House, I created a form to record the number of student volunteers so that enough food for the volunteers would be ordered. Also, during our school's major fundraiser, I developed a Google Form for students to record donations so that reports could be generated from the information more quickly than ever before. The possibilities of using Google Forms within a school environment are endless!

In this chapter, you will explore the following topics:

- Creating an assignment with Google Forms
- Installing the Flubaroo Google Sheets add-on
- Assessing an assignment with Flubaroo

Creating a Google Form

Since Google Forms is not as well known as apps such as Gmail or Google Calendar, it may not be immediately visible in the App Launcher. To create a Google Form, follow these instructions:

1. In the App Launcher, click on the **More** section at the bottom:

2. Click on the Google Forms icon:

3. If there is still no Google Forms app icon, open a new tab and type `forms.google.com` into the address bar.

4. Click on the **Blank** template to create a new Google Form:

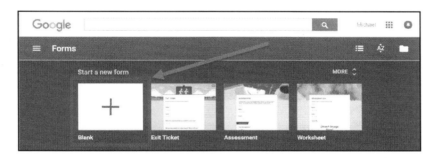

5. Google Forms has a recent update to Google's Material Design interface. This chapter will use screenshots from the new Google Forms look. Therefore, if you see a banner with **Try the new Google Forms**, click on the banner to launch the new Google Forms app:

6. To name the Google Form, click on **Untitled Form** in the top-left corner and type in the name. This will also change the name of the form. If necessary, you can click on the form title to change the title afterwards:

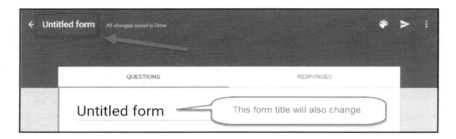

7. Optionally, you can add a description to the Google Form directly below the form title:

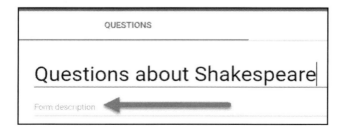

Often, I use the description to provide further instructions or information such as time limit, whether dictionaries or other reference books are permissible, or even website addresses to where they can find information related to the assignment.

Adding questions to a Google Form

By default, each new Google Form will already have a multiple choice card inserted into the form. In order to access the options, click on anywhere along the white area beside **Untitled Question:**

The question will expand to form a question card where you can make changes to the question:

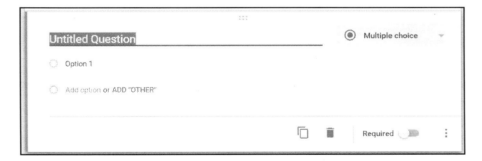

Type the question stem in the **Untitled Question** line. Then, click on **Option 1** to create a field to change it to a selection:

To add additional selectors, click on the **Add option** text below the current selector or simply press the *Enter* key on the keyboard to begin the next selector.

Because of the large number of options in a question card, the following screenshot provides a brief description of these options:

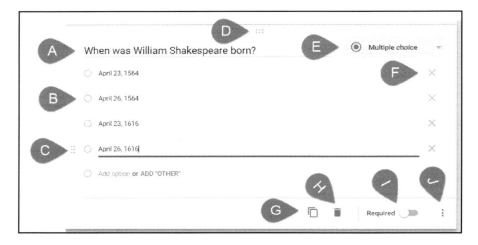

- **A**: Question title
- **B**: Question options
- **C**: Move the option indicator. Hovering your mouse over an option will show this indicator that you can click and drag to reorder your options.
- **D**: Move the question indicator. Clicking and dragging this indicator will allow you to reorder your questions within the assignment.
- **E**: Question type drop-down menu. There are several types of questions you can choose from. However, not all will work with the Flubaroo grading add-on. The following screenshot displays all question types available:

- **F**: Remove option icon.
- **G**: Duplicate question button. Google Forms will make a copy of the current question.
- **H**: Delete question button.
- **I**: Required question switch. By enabling this option, students must answer this question in order to complete the assignment.
- **J**: More options menu. Depending on the type of question, this section will provide options to enable a hint field below the question title field, create nonlinear multiple choice assignments, and validate data entered into a specific field.

Flubaroo grades the assignment from the Google Sheet that Google Forms creates. It matches the responses of the students with an answer key. While there is tolerance for case sensitivity and a range of number values, it cannot effectively grade answers in the sentence or paragraph form. Therefore, use only short answers for the fill-in-the-blank or numerical response type questions and avoid using paragraph questions altogether for Flubaroo graded assignments.

Once you have completed editing your question, you can use the side menu to add additional questions to your assignment. You can also add section headings, images, YouTube videos, and additional sections to your assignment. The following screenshot provides a brief legend for the icons:

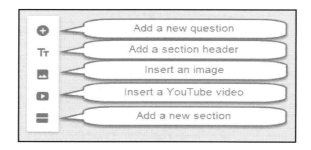

To create a fill-in-the-blank question, use the short answer question type. When writing the question stem, use underscores to indicate where the blank is in the question. You may need to adjust the wording of your fill-in-the-blank questions when using Google Forms. Here is an example of a fill-in-the-blank question:

Before romances were a genre, Shakespeare's romantic plays were called _____ to indicate that it was a mix of the two current genres. The missing word is

≡ Short answer

Short answer text

Identifying your students

Be sure to include fields for your students name and e-mail address. The e-mail address is required so that Flubaroo can e-mail your student their responses when complete. Google Forms within GAFE also has an option which allows automatic collection of respondent's username in the Google Form settings, found in the gear icon. If you use the automatic username collection, you do not need to include the name and e-mail fields.

If you teach a specialization such as a second language or a science such as chemistry, check out `Chapter 9`, *Customizing to Your Subject*, for helpful tips and third-party add-ons that can add functionality to your forms.

Changing the theme of a Google Form

Once you have all the questions in your Google Form, you can change the look and feel of the Google Form. To change the theme of your assignment, use the following steps:

1. Click on the paint pallet icon in the top-right corner of the Google Form:

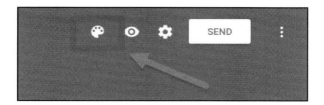

2. For colors, select the desired color from the options available. If you want to use an image theme, click on the image icon at the bottom-right of the menu:

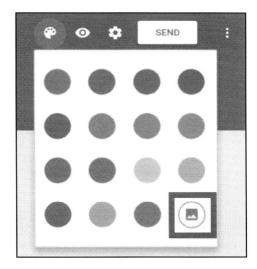

3. Choose a theme image. You can narrow the type of theme visible by clicking on the appropriate category in the left sidebar:

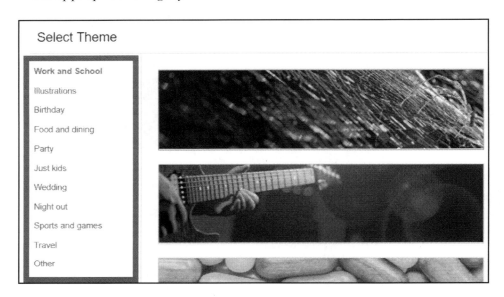

Another option is to upload your own image as the theme. Click on the **Upload photos** option in the sidebar or select one image from your Google Photos using the **Your Albums** option.

The application for Google Forms within the classroom is vast. With the preceding features, you can add images and videos to your Google Form. Furthermore, in conjunction with the Google Classroom assignments, you can add both a Google Doc and a Google Form to the same assignment. An example of an application is to create an assignment in Google Classroom where students must first watch the attached YouTube video and then answer the questions in the Google Form. Then Flubaroo will grade the assignment and you can e-mail the students their results.

Assigning the Google Form in Google Classroom

Before you assign your Google Form to your students, preview the form and create a key for the assignment by filling out the form first. By doing this first, you will catch any errors before sending the assignment to your students, and it will be easier to find when you have to grade the assignment later. Click on the eye-shaped preview icon in the top-right corner of the Google form to go to the live form:

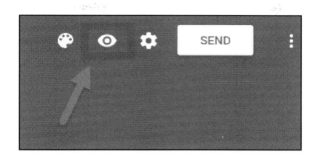

Fill out the form with all the correct answers. To find this entry later, I usually enter KEY in the name field and my own e-mail address for the e-mail field. Now the Google Form is ready to be assigned in Google Classroom. In Google Classroom, once students have submitted a Google Form, Google Classroom will automatically mark the assignment as turned in. Therefore, if you are adding multiple files to an assignment, add the Google Form last and avoid adding multiple Google Forms to a single assignment. To add a Google Form to an assignment, follow these steps:

1. In the Google Classroom assignment, click on the Google Drive icon:

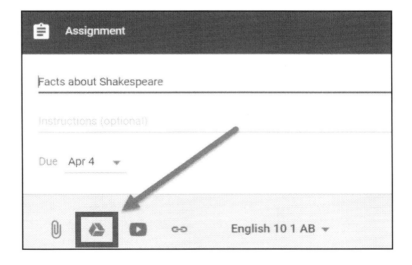

2. Select the Google Form and click on the **Add** button:

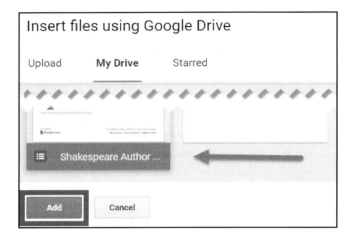

3. Add any additional information and assign the assignment.

Installing Flubaroo

Flubaroo, like Goobric and Doctopus, is a third-party app that provides additional features that help save time grading assignments. Flubaroo requires a one-time installation into Google Sheets before it can grade Google Form responses. While we can install the add-on in any Google Sheet, the following steps will use the Google Sheet created by Google Forms:

1. In the Google Form, click on the **RESPONSES** tab at the top of the form:

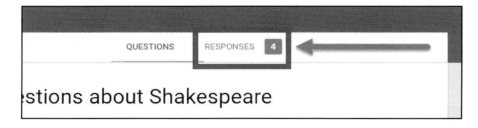

2. Click on the Google Sheets icon:

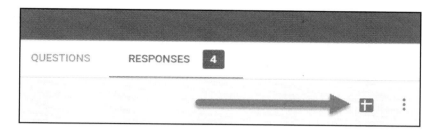

3. A pop-up will appear. The default selection is to create a new Google Sheet. Click on the **CREATE** button:

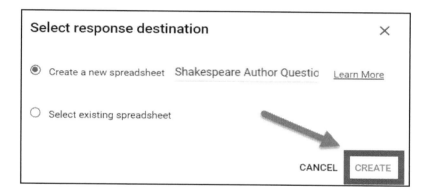

4. A new tab will appear with a Google Sheet with the Form's responses. Click on the **Add-ons** menu and select **Get add-ons...**:

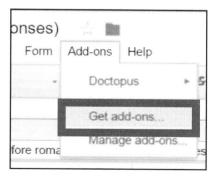

5. Flubaroo is a popular add-on and may be visible in the first few apps to click on. If not, search for the app with the search field and then click on it in the search results:

6. Click on the **+FREE** button:

7. The permissions pop-up will appear. Scroll to the bottom and click on the **Allow** button to activate Flubaroo:

8. A pop-up and sidebar will appear in Google Sheets to provide announcements and additional instructions to get started:

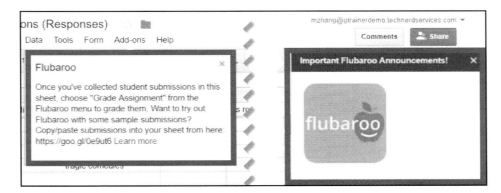

Assessing using Flubaroo

When your students have submitted their Google Form assignment, you can grade them with Flubaroo. There are two different settings for grading with it—manual and automatic. Manual grading will only grade responses when you initiate the grading, whereas automatic grading will grade responses as they are submitted.

Manual grading

To assess a Google Form assignment with Flubaroo, follow these steps:

1. If you have been following along from the beginning of the chapter, select **Grade Assignment** in the Flubaroo submenu of the **Add-ons** menu:

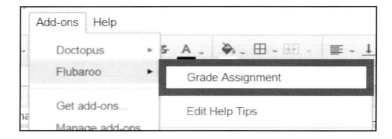

2. If you have installed Flubaroo in a Google Sheet that is not the form responses, you will need to first select **Enable Flubaroo in this sheet** in the Flubaroo submenu before you will be able to grade the assignment:

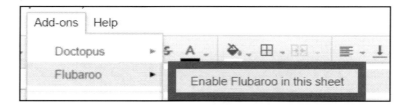

3. A pop-up will guide you through the various settings of Flubaroo. The first page is to confirm the columns in the Google Sheet. Flubaroo will guess whether the information in a column identifies the student or is graded normally. Under the **Grading Options** drop-down menu, you can also select **Skip Grading** or **Grade by Hand**. If the question is undergoing normal grading, you can choose how many points each question is worth. Click on the **Continue** button when all changes are complete:

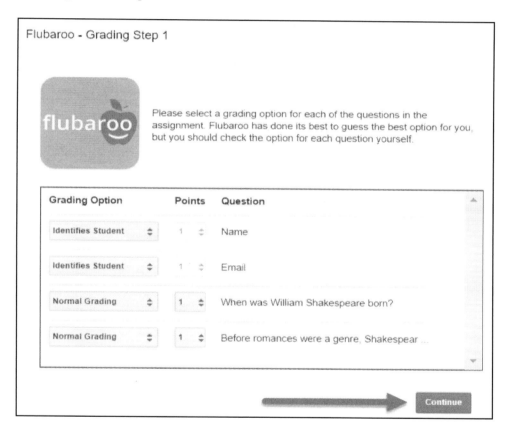

In my experience, Flubaroo accurately guesses which fields identify the student. Therefore, I usually do not need to make changes to this screen unless I am skipping questions or grading certain ones by hand.

4. The next page shows all the submissions to the form. Click on the radio button beside the submission that is the key and then click on the **Continue** button:

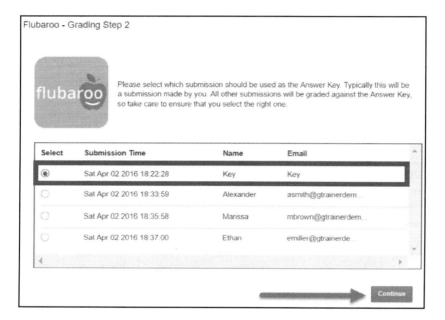

5. Flubaroo will show a spinning circle to indicate that it is grading the assignment. It will finish when you see the following pop-up:

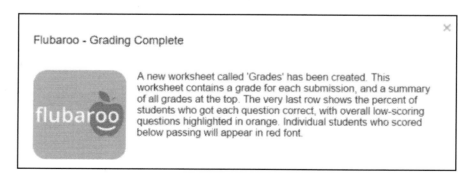

6. When you close the pop-up, you will see a new sheet created in the Google Sheet summarizing the results. You will see the class average, the grades of individual students, as well as the individual questions each student answered correctly:

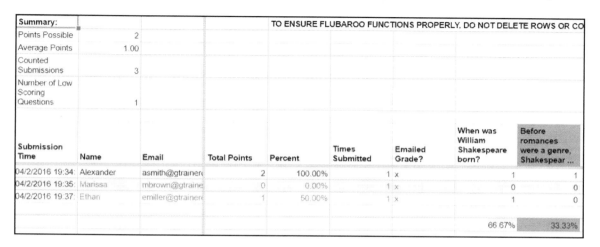

7. Once Flubaroo grades the assignment, you can e-mail students the results. In the **Add-ons** menu, select **Share Grades** under the Flubaroo submenu:

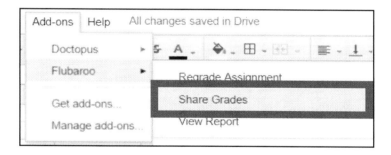

8. A new pop-up will appear. It will have options to select the appropriate column for the e-mail of each submission, the method to share grades with the students, whether to list the questions so that students know which questions they got right and which they got wrong, whether to include an answer key, and a message to the students. The methods to share grades include e-mail, a file in Google Drive, or both. Once you have chosen your selections, click on the **Continue** button:

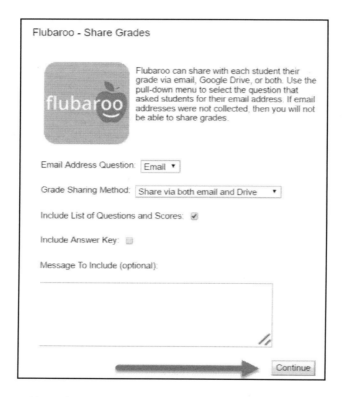

9. A pop-up will confirm that the grades have successfully been e-mailed.

Google Apps has a daily quota of 2,000 sent e-mails (including those sent in Gmail or any other Google app). While normally not an issue, if you are using Flubaroo on a large scale, such as a district-wide Google Form, this limit may prevent you from emailing results to students. In this case, use the Google Drive option instead.

If needed, you can regrade submissions. By selecting this option in the Flubaroo submenu, you will be able to change settings, such as using a different key, before Flubaroo will regrade all the submissions.

Automatic grading

Automatic grading provides students with immediate feedback once they submit their assignments. You can enable automatic grading after first setting up manual grading so that any late assignments get graded. Or you can enable automatic grading before assigning the assignment. To enable automatic grading on a Google Sheet that has already been manually graded, select **Enable Autograde** from the **Advanced** submenu of Flubaroo, as shown in the following screenshot:

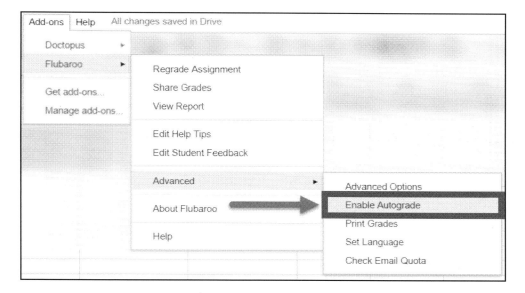

A pop-up will appear allowing you to update the grading or emailing settings that were set during the manual grading. If you select no, then you will be taken through all the pop-up pages from the *Manual grading* section so that you can make necessary changes.

If you have not graded the assignment manually, when you select **Enable Autograde**, you will be prompted by a pop-up to set up grading and emailing settings, as shown in the following screenshot. Clicking on the **Ok** button will take you through the setting pages shown in the preceding *Manual grading* section:

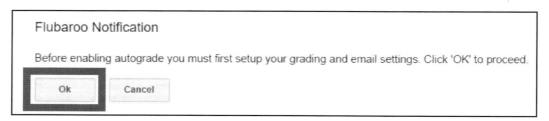

Tips and tricks when creating Google Form assignments

Now that you have created a Google Form and graded it with Flubaroo, there are several additional settings in Google Forms that are beneficial for using it in the classroom. Here are ten tips and tricks that you can use when creating Google Form assignments and exams for your students:

1. Once the Google Form creates a Google Sheet for the responses, you can navigate directly to the Sheet within the Assignment post in Google Classroom:

2. You can choose whether to make the Google Form accessible to anyone or limit it to users within the school district. The drop-down menu to change this setting is found within the Settings gear of the Google Form. Be sure to click on the **Save** button at the bottom of the **Settings** pop-up:

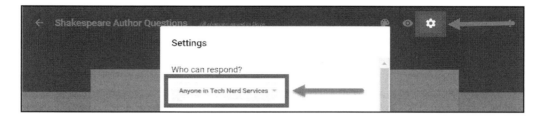

3. By default, students can submit the form multiple times. Flubaroo will display the most recent student submission in the Grades sheet, and Google Classroom will mark the assignment turned in after the first submission. While this feature may be useful so that students have an opportunity to achieve a higher grade if they redo the assignment, you may want to prevent them from resubmitting the form. For example, if you use a Google Form as a quiz, in the Settings gear you can check the checkbox beside **Can submit only 1 response (requires login)**.

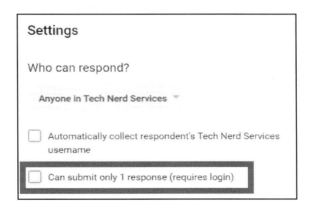

4. Google Forms can shuffle the order in which the questions appear. This feature can help prevent students from copying a classmate's answers. When creating your Google Form, place questions in their own section. (If you have multiple questions that reference the same information, place them all in a single section.) By checking the checkbox beside **Shuffle question order**, when students complete the assignment, Google Forms will shuffle the order of the sections:

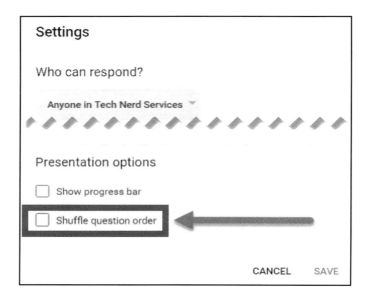

When using this selection, have the Google Form automatically collect the student's username, or the name and e-mail fields will be shuffled within the rest of the questions within the assignment.

5. Similar to shuffling the question order, you can shuffle the selections within a multiple choice question. In the More options menu of the question card, select **Shuffle option order:**

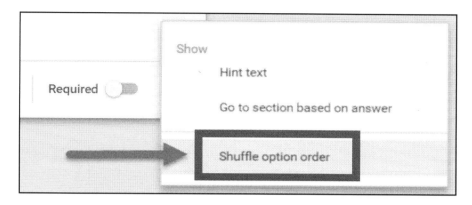

6. Another feature of multiple choice and drop-down question types is having specific selections navigate the student to a different question. For example, if a student chooses the correction selector, they will go to a harder question, but if they get the question wrong, they will go to an easier question. You will need to create each question in its own section and select **Go to section based on answer** in the more options menu of the question card. Then each selector will have a drop-down menu to choose where the student must navigate to next. You can even have a selector submit the form:

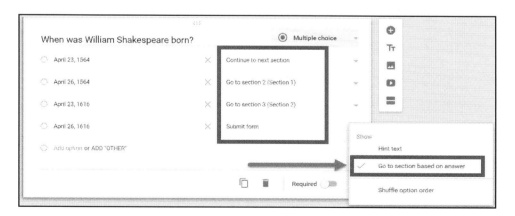

7. Data validation in short answer questions can confirm whether the entry matches a specific pattern, such as an e-mail or URL. This feature is found in the More options of the question card:

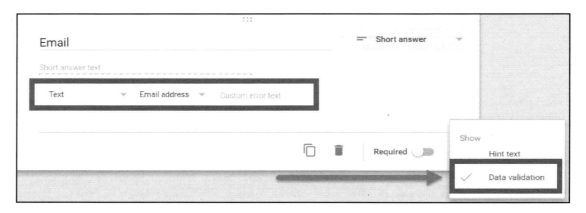

8. Another application of data validation is password protecting your Google Form. In the data validation settings of a short answer, change the validation type to **Regular expression** that matches a pattern. The pattern field will be the password. To ensure the password is exact, begin the password with ^ and end it with $. Whatever is between the two symbols will be the password. For example, the correct password for **^cookies$** is cookies. Set the question to a **Required** question and place it in its own section at the start of the Google Form. Users will not be able to continue until they input the correct password:

I have password protected my Google Forms for quizzes and exams so that students cannot start early. It also prevents students who are not in class to access the Google Form. Once the quiz or exam is complete, I disable **Accepting Responses** in the **Responses** tab of the form.

If you choose to use this feature in your Google Forms, you will not be able to shuffle the question order because the password section may not be the first section the students will see.

9. You can change the text that appears on the confirmation page once the form is submitted. If you place a URL in this section, students will be able to click on it. The confirmation page settings is found in the Settings gear:

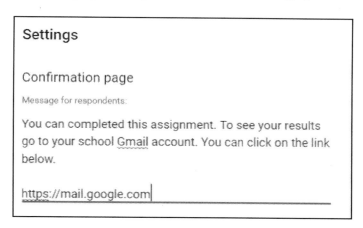

10. Google Forms also contains add-ons! You can explore additional third-party add-ons that can enhance your forms. To open add-ons, click on the **Add-ons...** selection in the Google Forms more options menu:

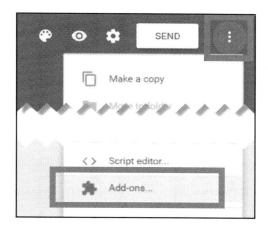

Summary

In this chapter, you learned how to create a Google Form, assign it in Google Classroom, and grade it with the Google Sheet's Flubaroo add-on. Using all these apps to enhance Google Classroom shows how the apps in the GAFE suite interact with each other to provide a powerful tool for you. Not only does Google Forms allow you to create and assign multiple choice and fill-in-the-blank questions, you now have tips to shuffle question order, password protects your forms, and ensure students only submit the form once.

With Google Forms, your Google Classroom assignments can include non-linear question orders, multiple opportunities for students to demonstrate understanding, immediate feedback, and automatic grading.

What began as a chapter to save time on grading multiple choice and fill-in-the-blank questions also provides tools to expand the types of assignments you can give your students. Google Classroom no longer only manages assignments, but it can also manage quizzes and exams.

With grading assignments in Google Classroom complete with Google Docs, Doctopus, and Goobric from the previous chapter, and Google Forms and Flubaroo in this one, in the next chapter we will explore how Google Calendar and Google Sites can help easily communicate the information within Google Classroom to parents.

Flubaroo was created by Dave Abouav, a Googler who developed Flubaroo in his free time as a free tool to help teachers. Dave was motivated to create Flubaroo from his experiences teaching evening physics classes at his local community college. He can be reached at dave@edcode.org.

More information about Flubaroo's features is available at http://www.flubaroo.com.

8
Keeping Parents in the Loop

Google classroom shines when it comes to organizing information between the teachers and students. Until recently, it did not provide a method for parents to reap its benefits. Now Google Classroom is able to send e-mail summaries to parents invited as guardians within Google Classroom. This method must be enabled by the school or district's IT department. If your school or district uses another method to communicate with the parents, they may leave this feature disabled because of its inherent security risks. (For example, my current school employer disables Google Classroom's guardian e-mails so that e-mails can undergo a verification process within an in-house system.) If your school does not allow guardian e-mails, by using Google Calendar, you are still able to inform them about important due dates from Google Classroom. Back in `Chapter 1`, *Getting to Know Google Classroom*, I mentioned that each class created in Google Classroom has a Google Calendar created for the question and assignment due dates. This chapter will explore how to use guardian e-mails within Google Class and the class' Google Calendar to communicate with parents and guardians.

 For the rest of this chapter, the term parents will refer to both parents and guardians.

Before diving into this topic, note that each school district is different in how it provides information to parents. Therefore, you may have to adapt the information you find in this chapter to best suit your school district's online resources. For example, in my school district, administrators, teachers, parents, and students are all included in an intranet designed for communication between stakeholders. Not only is there classroom-specific information, but the school can also place announcements of major events and deadlines to this intranet. I have also worked in school districts where the only means of communication with parents is with the school website. Therefore, this chapter will explore how to use the guardian e-mails feature and two different methods for keeping parents in the loop with

Google Calendar—with the calendar website and using Google Sites to create a class-specific website.

In this chapter, we will cover the following topics:

- Enabling and inviting parents to receive notifications from Google Classroom
- Activating sharing for the Google Calendar and identifying its website URL
- Creating a Google Site and adding the Google Calendar gadget to the web page
- Adding additional events to Google Calendar

Inviting parents to receive guardian e-mails

Guardian e-mails provide parents within daily or weekly e-mails summaries of upcoming assignment deadlines, announcements, and highlights outstanding assignments not yet turned in on Google Classroom. Parents must have a Google account in order to receive Google Classroom summaries. (The automated e-mail to the parent will provide instructions if the e-mail is not part of a Google account.) To enable and invite parents to receive guardian e-mails, use the following steps:

1. Click on the **STUDENTS** tab in the horizontal navigation of the class:

2. In the sidebar, click on the switch in the box titled **GUARDIAN EMAIL SUMMARIES**:

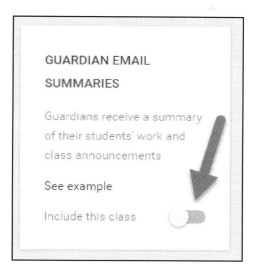

3. A dialog box will appear requesting confirmation. It will also have a checkbox to activate guardian e-mails in all of the other classes:

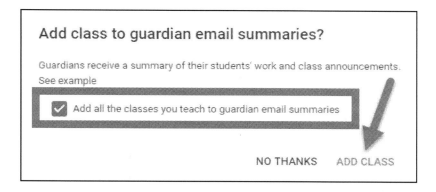

4. In the student list, click on **INVITE GUARDIANS** and enter the e-mail address of the guardian. Optionally, click on **ADD ANOTHER** if more than one guardian address is available. Once all e-mail addresses are entered, click on the **INVITE** button:

5. The e-mail address will display **(invited)** beside the guardian e-mail until the parent accepts the invitation as shown in the following screenshot:

6. Once the parent accepts the invitation, the parent's name will appear instead of their e-mail address as shown in the following screenshot:

If a parent uses an e-mail that is not linked to a Google Account, they will be redirected to an account creation page that can link their non-Google e-mail to an account:

For parents to access their e-mail notifications settings, direct them to Google Classroom's website, `classroom.google.com`. Google Classroom will display the student and allow them to change the frequency of receiving e-mail notification daily, weekly, or not at all. An example of the guardian settings is shown as follows:

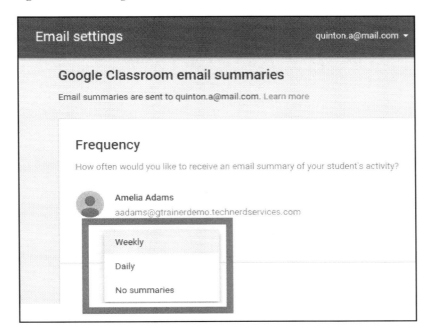

Sending e-mails to guardian e-mails manually

Guardian e-mails allow teachers to send an e-mail to all guardians within a class. A new **EMAIL ALL GUARDIANS** button appears at the top of the students list, shown in the following screenshot:

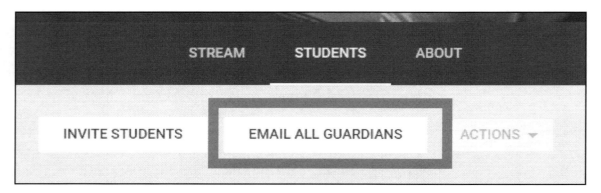

In addition, the three-dot menu beside each student in the student list contains options to e-mail the student's guardian, invite additional guardians, or remove current ones. An example of this menu appears in the following screenshot:

Sharing Google Calendar with a URL

Sharing the Google Calendar of a class is an alternative to the guardian e-mails if they are unavailable within your district. If your school district already has a web page or an intranet that connects the school with the parents, this method may be the simplest one to deploy. Since parents already have a website to go for school information, it is easy for them to find the link to your calendar on the school website. Before we include that link, we must make the calendars associated with your classroom public by following these steps:

1. In Google Classroom, navigate to the **ABOUT** section:

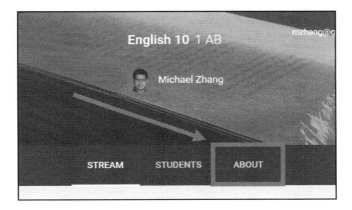

2. In the classroom details card, click on **Open in Google Calendar:**

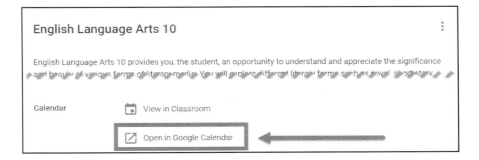

3. On the left sidebar, you will see a list of calendars. Hover your mouse over the calendar with the same name as your Google Classroom class and click on the drop-down menu:

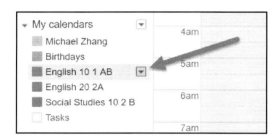

If you do not see a list of calendars under the **My Calendars** heading, click on the sideways triangle beside the heading as shown here:

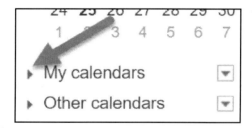

4. Click on **Share this Calendar:**

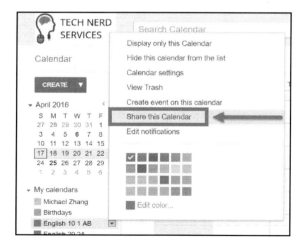

5. Under the **Share this calendar with others** checkbox, check the checkbox beside **Make this calendar public**. The drop-down menu beside this option should also be **See all event details**. In the following screenshot, all three checkboxes should be checked and **See all event details** should be selected in both the drop-down menus. Then click on the **Save** button:

Depending on the settings of your school's Google Apps, a dialog box may appear asking you to confirm the change to make the calendar public. Click on the **Yes** button to continue:

6. After saving, Google Calendar will exit settings. Click on the menu for the Google Classroom class calendar and select **Calendar settings**:

7. Scroll to the **Calendar Address** section and click on the **HTML** button:

8. A dialog box will appear with the URL to the Google Calendar as a website. Copy this URL and include it in your school's intranet or website:

Here is an example of the calendar in an Internet browser:

Now that you have the calendar URL, you can send it to whoever manages your school website, or add it to the school intranet. In my school district's intranet, I include the link in the homework section. I create an assignment that lasts until the end of the year and then include a message and the calendar link. The message usually explains to the parents that they can click on the calendar link to view their child's upcoming important dates for my class.

Adding your class's calendar to a parent's Google Calendar app
As part of the explanation to parents, I include instructions for them to add their child's Google Classroom calendar to their personal Google Calendar app. Parents with Google accounts, even the free *@gmail.com* accounts, can click on the **+ Google Calendar** button, shown as follows, at the bottom right-hand corner of the calendar website. This action should be done on a desktop computer:

Using Goo.gl to shorten the calendar URL

If you are displaying the calendar URL, such as in a printed newsletter, parents will have difficulty properly entering the long URL into the address bar of an internet browser. Therefore, you can use a URL shortener to redirect a short URL to your calendar. There are several URL shorteners on the internet; however, this example will use Goo.gl, Google's URL shortener tool. To shorten the Google Calendar URL, use the following steps:

1. In the calendar HTML address dialog box from the preceding step 8, right-click on the calendar URL and select **Copy link address**. If your web browser is not Google Chrome, the option may be worded differently:

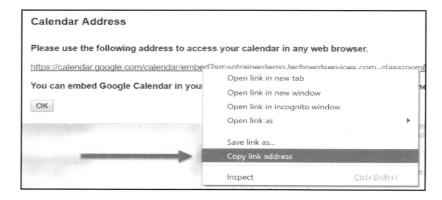

2. From the address bar of Google Chrome, navigate to goo.gl.
3. Paste your long URL in the field below **Paste your long URL here** and then click on the **Shorten URL** button:

4. The shortened URL will appear to the right of the **Shorten URL** button. A list of shortened URLs and their click analytics will appear below the long URL field. Use this new URL in your correspondence with parents online or in print:

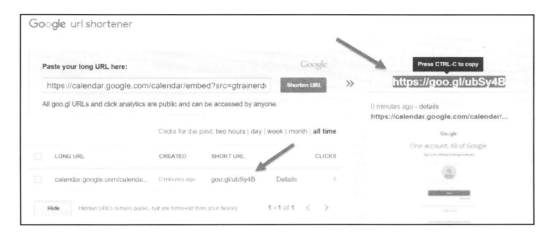

Simplify with short URLs
You can use URL shorteners for other website-based tasks. Not only is it easier for younger children to type in, you will also be able to see how many people are clicking on your link.

Creating a website for Google Calendar

If your school district does not have an easy method for communicating with parents online, you may need to use Google Sites to create a website for parents to access information from your class. Google Sites is a **WYSIWYG (what-you-see-is-what-you-get)** website editor that allows you to create websites without using code. While sending a link home with your students for a single calendar may be enough for your needs, Google Sites allows you to customize your Google Calendars, have multiple calendars visible on a single page, and make content from other Google Apps accessible to parents. Since this book focuses on Google Classroom, this section will provide steps to add the Google Classroom calendar to a Google Site. There is a plethora of other features found within Google Sites that are beyond the scope of this book. Use the following steps to create a Google Site:

1. Unless modified by your school IT, the App Launcher will not have an icon for Google Sites. Therefore, open Google Chrome and navigate to `sites.google.com`.
2. Click on the **CREATE** button in the sidebar:

3. On the next page, a **Blank template** is selected by default. Your school district may have site templates available in the **Browse the gallery for more** section. This example will use the **Blank template**. As you name the website, the site location fragment field will also fill. While optional, you can also modify this field afterwards to simplify the site URL:

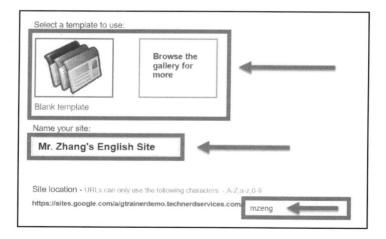

Site location URL endings are similar to house addresses in a city, there can only be one unique URL ending per school district. Therefore, if you receive an error when creating your site, try changing this field.

4. Scroll down and click on **Select a theme**. A menu will appear with several dozen themes for you to select. You can change a theme anytime in the future and further modify it to your liking. The default theme is **Ski:**

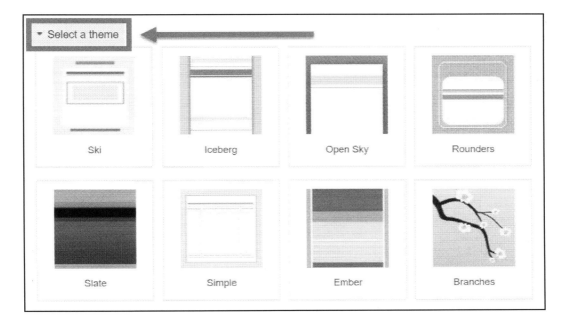

5. Once you have selected a theme, continue scrolling down and click on **More Options**. The **Site categories** and **Site description** fields will appear. These fields help search engines index your website so that it is easier to locate from search engines. Depending on whether you want your site to be easily found on the internet, you may choose to skip this step:

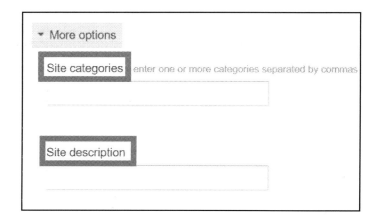

6. Click on the **CREATE** button at the top of the page:

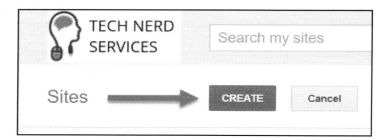

Your Google Site is now ready for your Google Classroom's calendar. You may choose to use Goo.gl to shorten your site's URL, as outlined in the previous section.

Adding a Google Calendar to a Google Site

Before adding a Google Calendar to your Google site, *your calendar needs to be public*. Use the steps found in the first half of this chapter to change this setting. Once your calendar is public, use these steps to add it to your Google Site:

1. Click on the edit page button in the heading of the site. The page will switch to edit mode:

2. In the **Insert** menu, select **Calendar** in the **GOOGLE** column:

3. In the dialog box that appears, check the checkbox beside the Google Classroom calendar. In this pop-up, you can select only a single calendar. You will be able to add additional calendars in the next step. Then, click on the **Select** button:

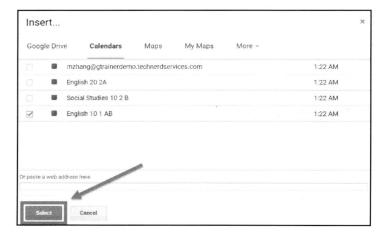

4. A new dialog box will appear with additional options for the calendar. A short description of each option is given after the following screenshot:

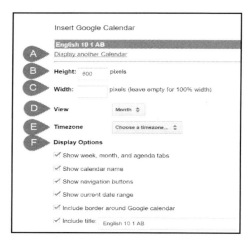

- **A**: **Display another Calendar** will take you to the previous dialog box to select an additional calendar.
- **B**: **Height** affects how tall the calendar appears on the web page.
- **C**: **Width** affects how wide the calendar appears on the web page. Leaving it blank will stretch the calendar to the left and right edges of the text box.
- **D**: **View** allows you to select whether you want the calendar to appear in the Month, Week, or Agenda views.

For smaller dimension calendars, I usually set the view of the calendar to Agenda view, which displays upcoming events as a list.

- **E**: **Timezone** will default to the viewer's time zone. This option will set the calendar to the specified time zone.
- **F**: **Display options** provide tabs and links within the calendar gadget that allows users to switch views and move the calendar forward or backward in time.

I usually remove most of the display options for calendars to simplify how viewers interact with the calendar. Especially, since many dimensions will make the month or week view unusable, removing the viewer's options to change these settings prevent them from having a poor experience.

5. Once you finalize all the options, click on the **SAVE** button. The dialog box will disappear:

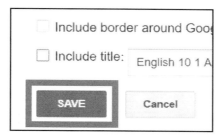

6. The page will display a gray box where the Google Calendar is on the web page, shown as follows:

However, the calendar content will appear after clicking on the **Save** button to exit the edit mode:

Your Google Classroom's calendar is now visible on a Google Site, as shown as follows. The final step is to make the Google Site visible so that parents and the public can view the site:

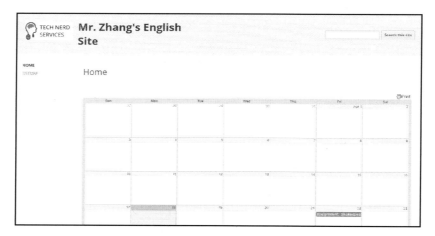

Sharing the Google Site

To make the Google Site visible to the public, use the following steps:

1. Click on the **Share** button:

2. Click on the **Change...** link on the first line below **Who has access**. This line will most likely be the school district's name:

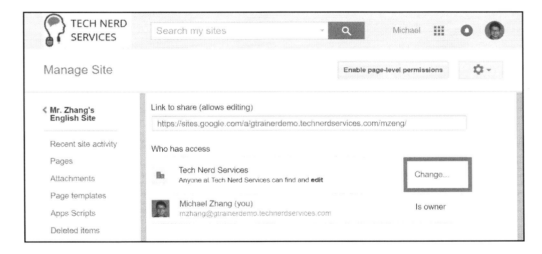

3. Select the radio button beside the **On – Anyone with the link** option. Then click on the **Save** button:

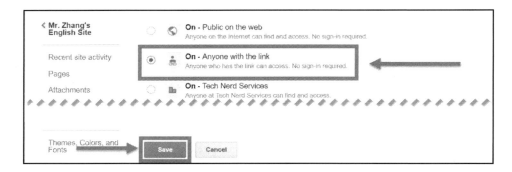

4. Copy and distribute the URL of the Google Site. Optionally, shorten the URL as described earlier in this chapter:

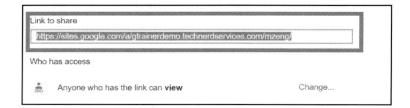

Creating additional events in Google Calendar

Communicating questions and assignment due dates may not be the only information you want to share with parents. In my class, I also include dates for quizzes and exams. Some teachers will add these to Google Classroom as an assignment so that they appear in the calendar automatically. However, you can also add them directly to Google Calendar as an event. While this feature is exclusively for the Google Calendar app, if parents are actively viewing the Google Calendar, this method may be a more efficient method for communicating information to both students and parents. There are several different methods to create an event in Google Calendar. The following steps will explore one method:

1. In the App Launcher, click on the **Calendar** icon. Another way to reach the Google Calendar app is to navigate to `calendar.google.com`:

2. Click on the **CREATE** button:

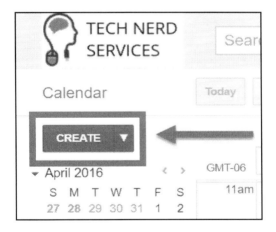

3. There are many settings for an event in Google Calendar. There are three settings that need changes for the event to be viewable on the Google Classroom calendar:

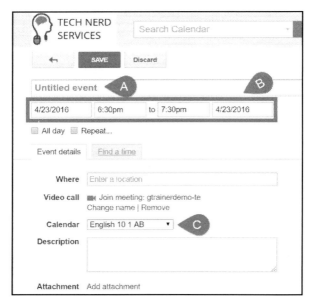

- **A**: The Title that parents and students will see
- **B**: The Date of the event
- **C**: The Google Calendar created by the class

4. Click on the **SAVE** button when all necessary changes have been made:

Adding more information to an event
Google Calendar allows you to add a description, location, attachments, and reminders to an event. If you incorporate Google Calendars into your communications strategy, consider exploring these and other features available through this app.

Summary

With guardian e-mails and Google Calendar, parents of your students will be able to view the Question and Assignment posts within your classes. While implementing either of these features may seem time-consuming to setup, this occurs at the beginning of the year or semester and requires little maintenance throughout the year. Now that you are able to invite parents or guardians to receive e-mail notifications, share the Google Classroom calendars with parents through a URL or a Google Site. Parents are able to actively engage with their student's assignments and assessments. Now that parents can view posts in Google Classroom, where you can manage and grade their assignments, it unifies much of the administration and management aspects of the classroom so that you can focus on teaching. The final chapter will explore subject specific third party apps that can enhance your activities within Google Classroom.

9

Customizing to Your Subject

Welcome to Google Classroom. Here you will explore how to set up Google Classroom and deploy it effectively in your classroom....

You're caught, aren't you?

If you have flipped to this chapter first, you are not alone. Even if you have been using Google Classroom and GAFE, I encourage you to start at the beginning. Jumping in near the end of the book means missing out on valuable tips and tricks on using Google Classroom and implementing it with other Google Apps. This chapter covers some extra tools to help with subject-specific needs. These will be more like finishing touches similar to icing flowers on a cake. Therefore, starting at this chapter may not provide you with the resources to effectively implement Google Classroom in your classes.

This chapter's format deviates from the rest of the book as it will showcase and reference some of the apps that I or my colleagues have used in our classes. Subjects that often cannot implement Google Classroom effectively are often limited to the features within GAFE. Here, we will explore native and third-party apps for English and social studies, second languages, science, and mathematics.

These extra features come from third-party apps and add-ons. Because this chapter focuses on providing suggestions for several subjects, only aspects of some of the apps will be explored. If a third-party feature interests you, take time to explore the full functionality of the apps, extensions, and add-ons. While some of these steps have been covered in previous chapters, this chapter will show how to add Google Chrome extensions and apps and add-ons in Google Docs. In addition, it will explore how to remove unwanted third-party add-ons.

In this chapter, we will cover the following topics:

- Managing citations for written assignments in English and social studies with Imagine Easy's EasyBib add-on
- Inserting letters with accents for second language classes using the Special Characters – Click and Paste add-on in Google Docs
- Creating and viewing 2D and 3D models of chemical compounds using the MolView app
- Creating math equations in Google Docs
- Plotting a graph in Google Docs using g(Math)
- Deleting Chrome Web Store apps and extensions and Google Docs add-ons

Citing references in Google Docs

With information becoming more and more readily available, properly citing sources is being taught to students at a younger age. English and social studies classes require a larger amount of writing with citations. While Google Docs provides inline citation, it does not offer a means to add a works cited page or a bibliography at the end of a document. Imagine Easy's Google Docs add-on, EasyBib provides this missing feature.

Using the research feature

The research sidebar in Google Docs allows students to use Google search for websites, images, and journal articles within the document. To enable and use its citation features, follow these steps:

1. In a Google Docs document, select the **Research** option in the **Tools** menu. The **Research** sidebar will appear on the right:

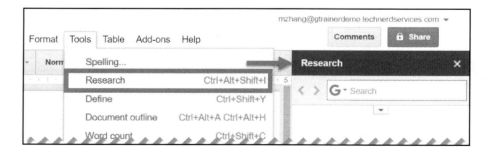

2. When hovering over the search results, three options will appear—**Preview**, **Insert Link**, and **Cite:**

- **A**: **Preview** shows a small window of the website beside the sidebar. Clicking on the window will open the website in a new window:

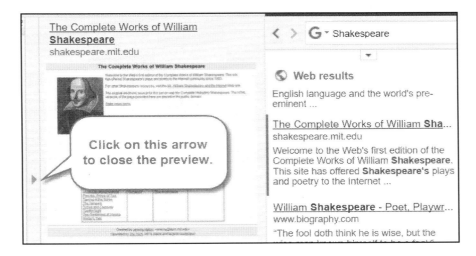

- **B**: **Insert Link** will paste a URL hyperlink into the document at the insertion point.

- C: **Cite** will add a number as a superscript at the insertion point and add the citation as a footnote to the page:

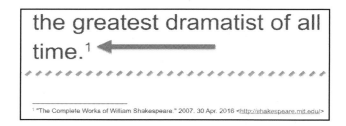

3. The default citation format is MLA, but this can be changed by clicking on the downward arrow below the search field, as shown in the following screenshot. APA and Chicago are the two other citation formats available.

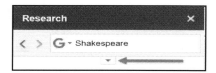

To change between various Google search categories (that is, Google images search, Google scholar, and so on), click on the search field to display the drop-down menu as shown in the following screenshot:

Creating citations with EasyBib

The **Research** tab can be useful regardless of whether inline citations are required for an English or social studies paper. However, many papers require a bibliography or a works cited page at the end of the paper. Follow these steps to enable and use Imagine Easy's EasyBib Google Doc add-on:

1. In a Google Docs document, select **Get add-ons...** from the **Add-ons** menu:

2. Because EasyBib is a popular add-on, you may be able to find it by scrolling through the available apps. If so, click on it to view more information about the app; otherwise, search for EasyBib in the search field:

3. Click on the **+FREE** button:

4. A pop-up appears with the permissions that EasyBib requires. Click on the **Allow** button and the pop-up will close:

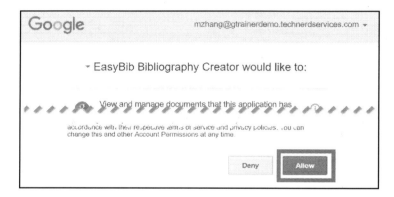

5. In the **Add-ons** menu of the Google Docs document, click on **Manage Bibliography** under the **EasyBib Bibliography Creator** submenu:

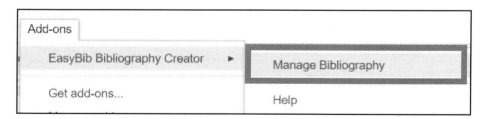

6. In the **EasyBib** sidebar, search for the reference. Once found, click on the **Select** button beside the desired source:

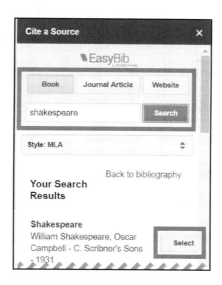

Continue adding sources to the bibliography in EasyBib. It will store them until ready to be added to the end of the document. When ready, click on the **ADD BIBLIOGRAPHY TO DOC** button below the style drop-down menu:

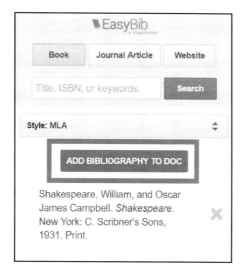

If EasyBib cannot find an appropriate source in the app, its website, `www.easybib.com`, can correctly format a source.

Add-ons in Google Sheets and Slides

Google Sheets and Forms have a plethora of add-ons available for data collection and processing. Explore their add-ons in their respective apps. Google Slides does not currently have add-ons, but will receive them in the future.

Adding letters with accents in Google Docs

When learning a second language such as French or Spanish, an extra challenge is to correctly insert letters with accents. Since most schools do not have special keyboard layouts for second languages, previous methods include memorizing key combinations or finding character maps on the computer to add an è. While many extensions and add-ons exist, the Special Characters – Click and Paste Chrome extension is a simple method of inserting accented letters regardless of the keyboard layout. To add this extension to Google Chrome or Chrome OS, follow these instructions:

1. In Google Chrome or on a Chromebook, open a new tab and click on the **Apps** icon in the bookmarks menu:

2. Click on the **Web Store** icon in the center of the screen:

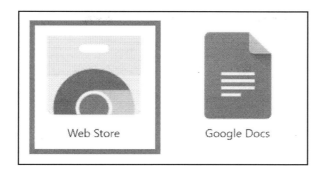

3. In the search bar, search for Special Characters – Click and Paste.
4. Under the **Extensions** section, click on **+ ADD TO CHROME:**

5. A pop-up will appear. Click on the **Add extension** button:

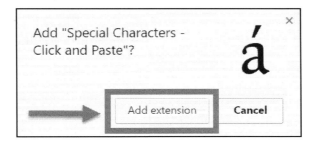

6. When installed, an icon for Special Characters will appear beside the omnibar:

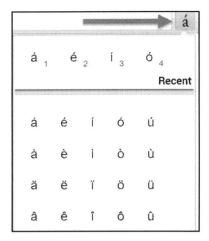

7. To insert a special character, click on the special character and then paste it into the text field of the Google Docs document.

Special Characters – Click and Paste was created by Benjamin Jones. Check out his other projects at `meteorfactory.io`.

Creating chemical models

For the sciences, many apps are available. One that stands out in its simplicity and use is MolView, a 2D and 3D chemical modeling app found in the Chrome Webstore. Use the steps from the previous section to install the app. Once installed, launch it from the apps page in Google Chrome or the App Launcher in Chrome OS.

A screenshot of the app is shown as follows:

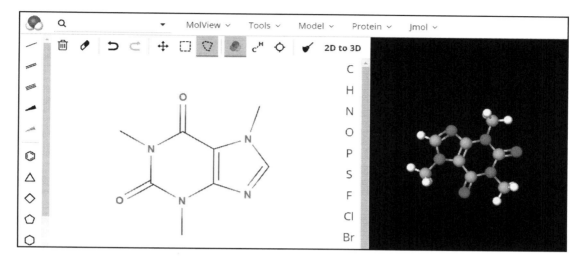

Students are able to create organic compounds and rotate the 3D representation so that it is viewable from multiple angles. Furthermore, using screen capture software such as the Chrome extension *Snagit* by Techsmith, it is possible to save these images and include them in activities and assessments.

Looking for a great biology app? Biodigital Human is a great app to explore the human body.

Inserting math equations in Google Docs

Mathematics is a greater challenge for integration than other subjects. With equations, charts, and graphs, creating or having students create math-related content in Google Docs can be a challenge. Google Docs has a built-in equation editor, but to plot graphs in Google Docs, the add-on g(Math) is required.

To create equations in Google Docs, follow these instructions:

1. In a Google Docs document, select **Equation** from the **Insert** menu:

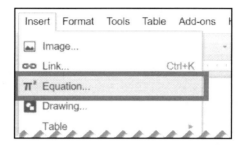

2. A blue rectangle around the insertion point indicates that the equation editor is active. Furthermore, an equation toolbar appears below the default toolbar:

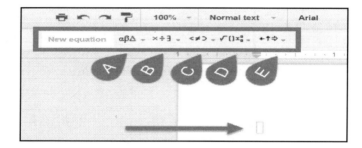

- **A**: Greek letters such as α
- **B**: Miscellaneous operations such as $\pm$
- **C**: Relations such as $\geq$
- **D**: Math operations such as fractions and square root
- **E**: Arrows

3. Insert special formatting and symbols from the equation toolbar to complete the equations. An example of the equation for the slope of a line is shown in the following screenshot:

$$m = \frac{rise}{run} = \frac{y_2 - y_1}{x_2 - x_1}$$

When using the equation editor, it is easier to begin with the formatting settings such as fractions and subscripts before adding in the text because it does not format previously entered text. Instead, the formatting buttons will create fields in the appropriate format to be filled in.

Plotting graphs in Google Docs

An add-on that can also create equations is g(Math). It uses the LaTex language to create images of equations, which can be pasted into a Google Docs document. g(Math) can also plot graphs in Google Docs. It needs to be installed as an add-on using the same instructions found in the *Creating citations with EasyBib* section at the start of this chapter. Once g(Math) is installed, use these steps to plot a graph:

1. Select **Create a graph** from g(Math)'s submenu:

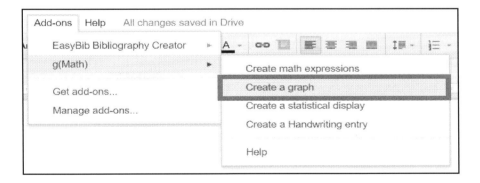

2. Enter the graph equation in the **Functions** field:

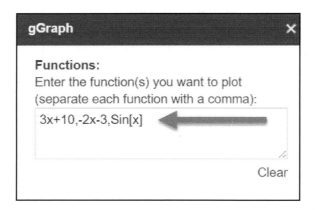

3. For additional mathematical constants, scroll down and click on the constants to insert them into a function. An screenshot of the list of constants and functions is shown as follows:

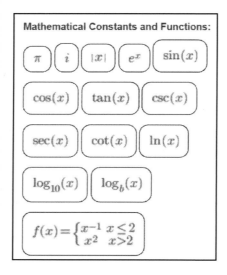

4. Scrolling to the bottom of the sidebar provides additional options such as plotting individual points on the graph, displaying the *y*-axis, and displaying grid lines:

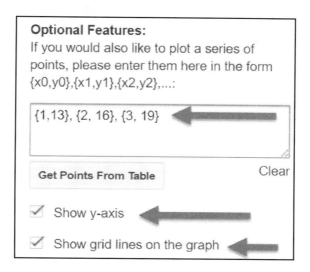

5. In the middle of the sidebar, there are **Graph Zoom Region** settings, which determine the domain and range of the graph. Select the maximum and minimum *x* and *y* values and their grid scales. When complete, click on the **Insert in doc** button:

6. An example of a graph created by g(Math) is shown in the following screenshot:

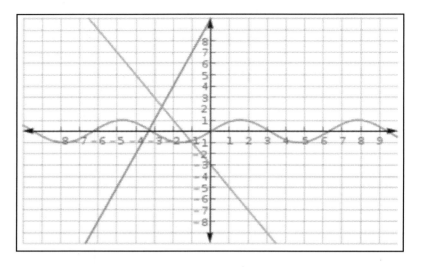

7. To edit a graph already inserted into a Google Docs document, click on the plot image and click on the **Edit from Doc** button in the g(Math) sidebar.

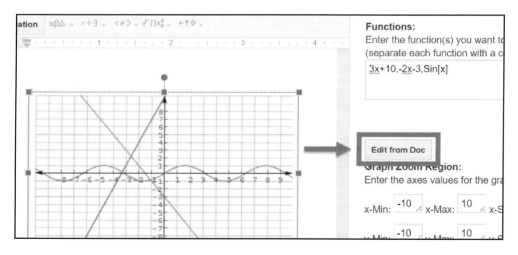

g(Math) was created by John McGowan and includes more features such as displaying statistical values and handwritten equations. Check out g(Math)'s website, www.gmath.guru, to find out more about this add-on.

Deleting apps, extensions, and add-ons

As you continue to explore different Chrome apps, extensions, and Google Docs add-ons, there will be ones that you try and decide not to use. Leaving those unused add-ons can slow down Google Chrome and Chrome OS. To maintain the best performance when using Google Apps, delete these unused apps, extensions, and Google Docs add-ons whenever possible.

Deleting Google Chrome apps and extensions follow similar steps. For apps, right-click on the **App** icon when viewing apps in Google Chrome or in the App Launcher of Chrome OS and select **Remove from Chrome...** as shown in the following screenshot:

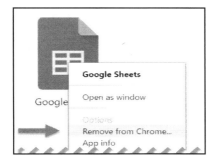

For deleting extensions, right-click on the extension icon beside the omnibar and select **Remove from Chrome...**.

Removing add-ons in Google Docs requires a couple of steps, which are as follows:

1. In Google Docs, select **Manage add-ons...** from the **Add-ons** menu:

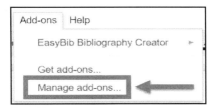

2. Beside the add-on, click on the **MANAGE** button and select **Remove:**

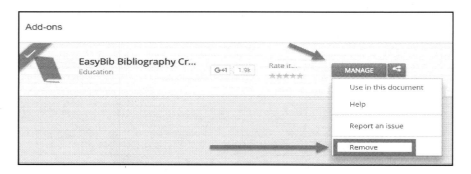

Exploring the Web Store by category

The Google Web Store can categorize the apps and extensions available. Great categories to explore are **Education** and **Productivity:**

In closing, I hope this book empowers you to explore, experiment, and grow with Google Classroom. As we teach that learning is lifelong, we too need to practice what we preach, and as we follow the ever-changing environment our students are learning in and adapt our teaching methods in meaningful ways, they will find relevance in our words.

Summary

Third-party apps allow you to customize your Google Classroom assignments to better fit your specific subject areas. This chapter explores several different methods of adding functionality to the core components of Google Chrome and Google Docs to enhance your Google Classroom experience.

This chapter not only provided several examples of third-party add-ons used in classes but also the steps for you to explore and find new features and functions. GAFE is a constantly changing learning system. As it improves, it is important to continue and explore the new changes that Google brings to this app suite.

Index

97376998R00141

Made in the USA
Columbia, SC
10 June 2018